Date Due

W/D

THE VILLAIN AS HERO
IN ELIZABETHAN TRAGEDY

THE VILLAIN AS HERO
IN ELIZABETHAN
TRAGEDY

By
CLARENCE VALENTINE BOYER, Ph.D.

NEW YORK / RUSSELL & RUSSELL

FIRST PUBLISHED IN 1914
REISSUED, 1964, BY RUSSELL & RUSSELL
A DIVISION OF ATHENEUM PUBLISHERS, INC.
BY ARRANGEMENT WITH
ROUTLEDGE & KEGAN PAUL, LTD., LONDON
L. C. CATALOG CARD NO: 64-15035
PRINTED IN THE UNITED STATES OF AMERICA

TO
MY WIFE
ETHEL PARKHURST BOYER
THIS BOOK
IS INSCRIBED

PREFACE

THIS essay, which was presented as a dissertation for the doctorate at Princeton University, is the result of an endeavour to discover whether or not the heroic criminals of Elizabethan tragedy adhered to any particular type. Investigation showed that the greatest villains were Machiavellians. But it did more ; it indicated that there were still other types of villains, and that many of them were not only heroic criminals, but were actually the protagonists of the plays in which their crimes were represented. This discovery changed the scope of my work, for it centred my attention upon the problem concerning the nature of tragic emotion, and interested me primarily in Aristotle's theory that tragic pleasure could not be aroused unless the character of the hero were good.[1] As the essay now stands, it is an attempt to trace back to Seneca the origin of plays in which the villain is hero ; to differentiate among the various types of villain-heroes presented by the Elizabethan dramatists ; to demonstrate the specific influence of Machiavelli upon the type, and to show the gradual breaking away from this influence ; and finally to analyse the nature of the emotion aroused by these villain-heroes, and to point out what is necessary to stimulate tragic pleasure when the hero is a villain.

Owing to the shortness of time at my disposal, I was

[1] In stating (pp. 2–3) that Aristotle's dictum that the absolute villain was unfit for the part of protagonist had apparently been accepted without objection, I neglected by an oversight to call attention to the fact that S. H. Butcher, in the essay following his translation of Aristotle's *Poetics*, has pointed out (pp. 313–16) the inadequacy of Aristotle's rules when applied to such a tragedy as *Richard III*.

forced to place somewhat arbitrary limits upon my work. For that reason I have treated no plays written by Beaumont and Fletcher, or by authors who began to write after the death of Shakespeare. For that reason, as well because a hasty examination led me to think that a careful study would not change the conclusions I had reached by other investigations, I have not considered Domestic Tragedy. Villain-heroines are also omitted, because it was my belief when I began to investigate that any conclusion a person might reach concerning the character of such women and the effect of such a type upon the emotions would involve a study of the psychology of the feminine mind apart from the study of villainy itself when found in the character of the protagonist. Finally, the absence of one other type of hero,—the conquering hero,—the type represented by Tamburlaine, must be noted. The conventional standard of judgment distinguishes between necessary and unnecessary cruelty in war, and also between warfare carried on for personal aggrandizement and that which is waged for a *cause;* but the difficulty of determining whether a representative audience would consider a given war as justifiable or unjustifiable, and the acts of a great warrior, in a specific case, as necessarily or unnecessarily cruel, seemed to me, when I was planning my thesis, to be great enough to justify me in ruling out the heroes of foreign conquest from the discussion. Wherever, therefore, the dramatist has confined his hero's activities to foreign conquest, I have refrained from criticism ; but wherever he has caused his hero to commit acts in civil life which are violations of the moral code—as in the case of Selimus—I have considered the tragedy within the scope of this work.

I desire to take advantage of this opportunity to acknowledge with gratitude my indebtedness to those who have assisted me in this undertaking. Professor Stockton Axson, formerly of Princeton, now of Rice Institute, Texas, helped me materially in outlining the work and in untangling many a knotty point along the way. I wish also to thank Professor T. H. Guild, of the University of Illinois, for time unselfishly devoted to reading the manuscript, and criticising both the method of presentation and the manner of expression. To Professor T. M. Parrott and Professor J. Duncan Spaeth, of Princeton, I am indebted in a manner and to a degree which I make no pretence of adequately acknowledging here. It is their stimulating suggestions, scholarly criticism, and unfailing kindness that have made the work possible.

URBANA, ILLINOIS,
          January, 1914.

CONTENTS

I

INTRODUCTION

II

SENECA

III

ENGLISH PLAYS BEFORE MARLOWE

IV

MACHIAVELLI

V

MARLOWE AND THE MACHIAVELLIAN VILLAIN-HERO

CONTENTS

PAGE

THE VILLAIN AS HERO

I

INTRODUCTION

ELIZABETHAN drama is a term rather loosely used to cover the plays produced between the accession of Elizabeth, in 1558, and the restoration of Charles II in 1660. The plays of this period are, as every student knows, of very mixed type and unequal value, including as they do the sacred drama of national origin, the Latin imitations of Plautus and Seneca, the masterpieces of Shakespeare, and the decadent drama immediately preceding the closing of the theatres. It was towards the end of the sixteenth century that the Moral plays, performed chiefly for the edification and amusement of the common people, and the stiff imitations of classical plays, performed chiefly at court, began to give way before a new movement drawing nourishment from both, but distinctly different from either— the Romantic Drama, the drama of passion, which was the crown and flower of Elizabethan dramatic art, and of which Shakespeare is the great exemplar.

The first author to make a lasting impression upon this drama through technical excellence as well as imaginative power was Marlowe. Mar-

lowe's influence was manifold. *Tamburlaine* stands
as a landmark—for its poetry, its power, and as a
forerunner of the conquering-hero type of play.
The Jew of Malta, also, which was produced soon
afterwards, was one of the most popular plays of
the day.[1] The character of Barabas, the hero of
this play, has been frequently discussed, not only
because of the interest of the play, but because in
the two or three following decades we meet time
and again with character-types clearly suggested by
Barabas. But the significance of the fact that
Barabas plays a double rôle, that we have here a
play with the villain as hero, seems to have escaped
general attention.

The paradoxical phrase " villain as hero " may
need explanation and definition. Satan has often
been called the real hero of *Paradise Lost*, but he
is never referred to as the *villain*—perhaps because
the use of that term is unusual in connection with
an epic. At any rate, the importance of the double
rôle seems not to have been noted in this case any
more than in *The Jew of Malta ;* and the writers
on the technique of the drama, and on tragedy in
general, have omitted to discuss the influence of
such a character-type upon dramatic construction,
and upon tragic emotion. Aristotle's dictum that

---

[1] Henslowe records thirty-six performances between Feb. 26,
1591–2 and June 21 (23), 1595–6. (Performed by Strange's men,
as an old play, Feb. 26, 1591–2, and thence till Feb. 1, 1593 ;
again by Sussex' men Feb. 4, 1593–4 ; again by Queen's and
Sussex' men April 3 and 7 (8), 1593–4 ; again by the Admiral's
men, May 14 ; again by the Admiral's and Chamberlain's men,
June 4 (6) and 13 (15) ; again by the Admiral's men, June 23 (25),
and thence till Dec. 9 (10), also after an interval, Jan. 9, 1595–6
to June 21 (23) ; in all thirty-six performances.—*Henslowe's
Diary*, ed. Greg, Part II, p. 151.)

the absolute villain was unfit for the part of protagonist because he would arouse neither pity nor fear,
has apparently been accepted without objection.[1]

In the following dissertation the terms *hero* and
protagonist[2] are used interchangeably, and by a
hero is meant the character who takes the chief
acting part in the play, and in whose actions,
mental states, and ultimate fortunes we are most
interested. It is only in this sense of a " star " or
" actor playing the leading rôle " that the word
hero is here used. The definition determines the
technical position the actor holds in the cast ; it
does not, nor is it intended to, define the character
of the hero. His character is usually good, but is not
necessarily so, as the title *Villain as Hero* indicates.

Before defining *villain* in the sense hereinafter to
be used, it may be well to consider the ideas ordin-
arily associated with the word. One usually thinks
of a villain as a man with something mean and low
in his disposition, and it is very difficult to dis-

---

[1] Professor George R. Noyes has an article—" Aristotle and
Modern Tragedy "—in *M.L.N.*, 1898, p. 12, in which he discusses four types of tragedy classed as weak by Aristotle.
Professor Noyes questions the soundness of Aristotle's defini-
tions, and cites *Richard III* and *Sejanus* as successful tragedies
representing the " fall of a bad man into adversity."

[2] The name " protagonist " was originally not limited to the
drama. " The ' protagonist ' was the principal contestant, the
champion, the leader, the bearer of the principal rôle in any
kind of action in which a contest or struggle of any sort was
involved." Soon after the introduction of the actors' contest in
449 B.C. those who competed were called αγωνισται, a term
borrowed from the athletic contests. Later all actors were called
αγωνισται, and then the best actors were distinguished by being
called πρωταγωνισται. And naturally those with the best
histrionic ability played the most important or sympathetic
parts.—Kelley Reese, " The So-called Rule of Three Actors in
the Classical Greek Drama." University of Chicago Thesis, 1908.

sociate this idea from the term itself. In the simplest conception, the hero of drama is a good man trying to accomplish some good end ; the villain is a bad man who, from hatred or for personal advancement, uses unjust means to block the hero's purpose. This is the position the villain usually occupies in comedy. But the character and relative position of hero and villain are not always so simple. As we look back over the field of serious tragedy—Greek, Roman, English—we see that there are certain plays in which a character comes into conflict with moral law, with man-made law, or with both. Sometimes it is the hero, sometimes the villain, occasionally both. Œdipus, for example, the hero of *Œdipus the King*, comes into conflict with moral law ; Antigone defies the laws of Creon ; and Creon himself, as villain, defies the moral law. Macbeth violates the laws of both God and man by treason and murder. As to whether the characters engaging in such conflict with law are to be regarded as heroes or as villains depends, as will be seen, upon the motive for the conflict. When the characters that come into conflict with law are subordinate, and when their machinations contribute to the overthrow of the hero, we recognize them immediately as villains, as e.g. Creon in Sophocles' *Œdipus Colonus*, Claudius in *Hamlet*, Goneril and Regan in *King Lear*. But there are plays in which the characters that come into conflict with law are the protagonists themselves, and where this conflict itself—and not its effect upon the fortunes of another—forms the centre of dramatic interest. Yet even in such cases the pro-

tagonists are not necessarily villains ; for a person
with a good character may come into conflict with
law, as did Œdipus and Antigone. In fact, Aristotle, drawing his conclusions from the best Greek
tragedies, lays it down as a rule that " in respect
of character there are four things to be aimed at.
First, and most important, it must be good. Now
any speech or action that manifests moral purpose
of any kind will be expressive of character ; *the
character will be good if the purpose is good.*"[1] It is
the hero's character that Aristotle is speaking of.
In another place[2] he makes more clear what he
understands by *good*. The character of the ideal
hero must not be bad, nor yet perfect, but " the
character between these two extremes—that of a
man who is not eminently good and just, yet whose
misfortune is brought about not by a vice or depravity, but by some error or frailty." For the
downfall of the utter villain,[3] although it " would
doubtless satisfy the moral sense, would inspire

[1] *Poetics*, XV, p. 53, Butcher's translation.
[2] *Ibid.*, XIII, p. 45.
[3] Aristotle seems to associate " vice and depravity " with
" utter " villainy, and to distinguish between these qualities and
" frailty." It is customary for us to do the same. " Vice is a
matter of habit in doing that which is low and degrading "
(*Cent. Dict.*), but a frailty may amount to a grand passion, such
as Othello's jealousy. Now it is perfectly true that if villainy
consisted only in doing that which was low and degrading we
could never sympathize with the villain ; his downfall would
never excite tragic emotion. It will be the object of this essay
to show, however, that a man may be a villain without being
low and degraded. Crime may make him a villain, but crime is
not necessarily degrading. And yet crime, wilful crime, cannot
be called an error or frailty. It is in cases where the villain's
downfall is brought about not by error or frailty, but by some
wilful violation of moral law, which violation, however, does
not sink to the level of vice or depravity, that Aristotle's dictum
that the downfall of the villain would not be tragic is questionable.

neither pity nor fear," actions which excite pity and fear being "the distinctive mark of tragic imitation."

Thus it may be seen that the conflict between character and moral law does not necessarily make a villain. On the contrary, we may say that when the conflict between character and law springs from inherent defects in the very nature of the individual, and is not simply a contest for some selfish end, the result is a tragic hero whose character conforms to Aristotle's definition of *good*. Aristotle himself names Œdipus as such an example.[1] In modern drama Lear, who acts fitfully and makes an error of judgment, and Othello, who acts blindly and passionately, may be cited. But when a character deliberately opposes moral law from wilfulness, and for the purpose of advancing his own interests, recognizing at the same time the sanction of the law he defies, we call him a villain.[2]

But a certain confusion is likely to arise when the protagonist defies what by common consent is regarded as the moral law, but what he refuses to acknowledge as the moral law. Such a character would be denominated to-day a Superman. The doctrine of the Superman, as I understand it, is a philosophy which teaches that there is no divine law or absolute moral standard ; that the strongest instinct in man is the " Will to Power " ; that he who has this instinct in the highest degree is most fit to rule ; that whatever such a man thinks is

---

[1] *Poetics*, XIII, p. 47.

[2] Antony in *Antony and Cleopatra* is not a villain because, although he knows what he is doing to be wrong, he is not trying to advance his own interests. On the contrary, he knows that he is acting against self-interest, but his passion masters his judgment.

right is right because he thinks it, i.e. such a man
is his own maker of values ; that the so-called
moral law is simply a code contrived by the weak
to protect them from the strong, and that it has
no divine authority whatsoever behind it.

Now a number of the villains of Elizabethan
tragedy are Supermen, but a Superman is not
necessarily a villain. Whether he is or not depends
upon *our* recognition of the sanction of the moral
law which he breaks, and his reason for breaking it.
Take Shaw's *Devil's Disciple*, for instance. The
hero of this play, it is said, defies the moral law, not
as a result of any inherent weakness or defect, but
consciously, wilfully, and deliberately. Yet this
man is not a villain. He lies and deceives (i.e.
breaks, apparently, the moral law), but he does so
to save Pastor Anderson's life. Shaw gains our
sympathy for him as hero, because his machinations
are actually used, not to advance self-interest, but
to save another at the expense of his own life.
Shaw's paradox is just this : Your true hero must
be a villain. But Shaw's aim is reconstruction of
our conception of moral law, and he is so far successful that the audience denies the paradox and
refuses to regard the hero's action as immoral.
Instead, the audience regards the Puritans as
narrow-minded. Lying and deceiving are usually
condemned because the purpose behind the act is
either cowardly, as e.g. when a man lies to save
himself ; or malicious, as when a man deceives to
injure others. But every one who applauds the
action of the Devil's Disciple tacitly admits that
there are circumstances when lying is justifiable.

The very fact that the hero of this play is justified in the eyes of the audience proves that the so-called moral law which he has broken is not recognized as universally binding. But let your Superman violate a law whose sanction we (the audience) recognize, and the fact that *he* does not recognize the sanction of the law he has broken will not prevent us from adjudging him a villain. Our recognition (not his) of the sanction of moral law has everything to do with the question.

We may say, then, that *a villain is a man who, for a selfish end, wilfully and deliberately violates standards of morality sanctioned by the audience or ordinary reader.* When such a character is given the leading rôle, and when his deeds form the centre of dramatic interest, the villain has become protagonist, and we have the type play with the villain as hero.

It will be seen that Barabas occupies precisely the position of villain-hero defined above. He is a criminal of the deepest dye ; he is guilty of treason, murder, and poisoning ; he commits his crimes wilfully and deliberately, and he is perfectly well aware that his acts are crimes. He commits crimes for revenge, because he hates Christians as such, and hates especially the men who have taken his gold. He probably also enjoys crime for crime's sake, and takes a keen relish in outwitting his adversaries. Barabas is such a superlative villain that he is usually spoken of as a monster. But he is also the hero of the play. Like *Tamburlaine, The Jew of Malta* is strictly a one-man play. The Jew is not only the centre of the action, but fairly monopolizes the action. Other characters are but slightly sketched in, and merely exist as tools or objects for the Jew to work with or upon. How shall such a unique dramatic creation be accounted for?

In the first place, there is a subjective side to this whole matter which cannot be neglected. Marlowe's own temperament was that of a "rebel," one that sympathized with open defiance of established authorities, recognized standards, and conventions. Barabas, Tamburlaine, and Faustus are all characters who, in the consciousness of their own superabundant power, override the barriers of human and divine restraint. Marlowe's attitude towards moral order is much the same as Nietzsche's. To Marlowe the moral law is simply constraint—restraint of individual genius—genius for pleasure or power. His heroes are Supermen whose "Will to Power" triumphs over every other consideration, and justifies them to themselves. Their wickedness is their strength: without it they are nothing.

Marlowe's temperament, however, does not satisfy all our queries about *The Jew of Malta*. The question naturally arises: Out of what materials did Marlowe construct his villain-hero? It seems very probable that *The Jew of Malta* was founded upon the actual career of a notorious Jew of the sixteenth century—Josef Nassi[1]—who maintained political and financial relations with Spain and France, and later showed himself the enemy of both countries; who really possessed through his alliances that trade power of which Barabas boasts;

[1] Cf. L. Kellner, "Die Quelle von Marlowe's 'Jew of Malta,'" *Eng. Stud.*, Vol. X.

and who finally with the help of the Turks and that
of the crown prince, whose name was Selim, actually
became the ruler of a Christian island. But there
is wanting any connected account, any written
" story " of the career of Josef. And even if we
admit the romantic interest of such material as
existed, it alone does not explain the creation of
such a figure as Barabas. Why should Marlowe
make a romantic hero an out-and-out villain, even
if he himself saw virtue in villainy ? It was a daring
experiment unless there was something in the air
to make him feel that such a figure would prove
fascinating when staged.

As a matter of fact, the air was charged with
suggestion. We can best explain Barabas by first
accounting for the scenes of horror whose atmosphere permeated almost the entire tragic drama of
the sixteenth century. These scenes reflected in a
general way the spirit of the times, and mirrored
the impression made upon Elizabethan minds by
the pictures of abuse of power and dire revenge
represented in the chronicles of England's past.
But more specific was the influence of Machiavelli,
with whose name was associated a haunting apprehension of guileful wickedness prevailing over innocent simplicity.[1] And finally, Seneca must be
reckoned with in accounting for both the sombre
setting of the plays of this period and the particular
type of play with the villain as hero.

In considering the spirit of the times as a stimulus
to the kind of tragedy written by Marlowe and his

[1] Lewis Campbell, *Tragic Drama in Æschylus, Sophocles and
Shakespeare*, pp. 60–1 (1904).

contemporaries, an important place must be given to the daily events of that stirring period. It was a time when the imagination of men thrilled to the tales of wildest adventure, boundless courage, and bloody deeds. Piracy prevailed upon the high seas, quick and brutal passions were the rule at home. " Drake in his cabin drinking and praying with the unmoved lieutenant whom he was to hang the next day is a bit of fact that rivals in horror the devilries of a Barabas."[1] Violence found a place in the lives of even the most literary and intellectual of men : Jonson killed his man, and Marlowe was slain in a drunken brawl. It is not strange that scenes of lawlessness and bloodshed appealed to playwrights who were themselves duelists. It was a time when the national consciousness was being most deeply stirred ; everywhere the passionate and the heroic were the rule, not the exception ; the drama did but reflect contemporary life and manners. Civil war was raging in France. Deadly hatred prevailed between Huguenot and Catholic ; assassination was no uncommon means of removing enemies ; and the Massacre of St. Bartholomew equalled in horror anything the mind was capable of imagining. In Italy court intrigue, a policy of deceit, ruthless murder, and undying revenge existed side by side with the highest culture and most brilliant attainments. The scandalous life of the popes and cardinals was notorious. The names of Alexander VI and Cæsar Borgia were bywords for simony, adultery, incest, and murder. Now, Englishmen were familiar with the history of

[1] Thorndike, *Tragedy*, p. 79.

monarchical Europe, with the life of Italy, France, and Spain, if not through travel—which was very general—at least through literature. And if the conditions of the Latin nations did not prevail in England in their worst features, they at least exerted a tremendous influence on manners and art, so that the sensational life of Italy and France may be considered as a part of the spirit of the times which influenced the work of Marlowe and his dramatic associates.

Going back one generation in their own history the playwrights came upon the martyrdoms of the reign of Queen Mary. They had only to turn to the chronicles to become familiar with blood and violence, the extinction of royal families, the boundless ambition of individual barons that marked the conduct of the War of the Roses. Going back still further to the legendary history of Britain they still met with such cruelty, faithlessness, and unlawful passions as are associated with the names of Lear, Arthur, and Locrine. Wherever the dramatist turned, aggressive self-assertion, wanton crime, and remorseless villainy seemed to be as much a part of man's nature as modest heroism, misled righteousness, or erring passion. As our dramatists aimed at impartial consideration and presentation of every salient motive and every prominent feature in man's experience, the life represented upon the stage of that era was necessarily one in which horror and violence were prominent. And then, as if to sanction the instinct to dramatize man's villainy, there was the ever present, the approved example of the classic Seneca.

II

SENECA

THE influence of Seneca on Elizabethan drama has
been carefully though not exhaustively studied,[1]
so that there is general agreement as to the fact,
if not the extent of his influence. To Seneca is
usually attributed the introduction of the ghost
and the chorus, the division of the play into five
acts, as well as the introduction of various themes,
such as revenge. It is the question of themes and
the manner of treating them that concerns us here.
All of Seneca's themes are violent and sensational.
It is true that with the exception of *Octavia* they
are taken from Greek sources, but owing to the
manner of treatment they radiate anything but a
Greek atmosphere. In the selection of characters,
Seneca is faultless. Even Aristotle might be said
to approve his choice, for the Greek critic remarks :
" The best tragedies are founded on the story of a
few houses—on the fortunes of Alcmæon, Œdipus,
Orestes, Meleager, Thyestes, Telephus, and those
others who have done or suffered something terrible."[2] But in the general management of his
subjects, Seneca makes many of these tragedies
not terrible, but shocking, horrible, revolting ;

[1] Cf. Thorndike, Cunliffe, etc.
[2] Butcher's translation, p. 47.

13

hence they do not produce tragic pleasure. Revenge is, indeed, the impelling force which drives many of Seneca's characters to their monstrous deeds; but revenge is not, as some critics maintain, always represented by him as a sacred duty, as it came to be later on in Elizabethan drama, in the *Hamlet* type of play, for instance. It may be the death of a relative for which vengeance is sought, and the revenge may be associated with some supernatural force, as e.g. the ghost. But the ghost, in *Thyestes* at any rate, does not appear to urge Atreus to revenge as a sacred duty; on the contrary, it urges him to revenge that both he and Thyestes may suffer for their wickedness and that of their ancestors. The revenge itself is represented as sinful; it is undertaken for personal injuries, and is born of malice rather than of duty.

In thus representing faithlessness, cruelty, murder, revenge, and lust as governing the hearts and minds of men in high places—even in his appeal to magic and the supernatural[1]—Seneca offered themes both familiar and pleasing to the audiences of the Elizabethan theatre. At the same time Seneca stood for antiquity, and his name, technic, and moralizing passages exerted a paramount influence with the classicists. Now among the plays of this authoritative and highly appreciated dramatist we find two that clearly suggest the villain-hero type, viz. *Medea* and *Thyestes*.[2] Considering the re-

---

[1] Cf. the poisoned robe of Hercules, and the art of Medea.

[2] Clytemnestra comes near being the protagonist in Seneca's *Agamemnon*. This is because she is so well psychologized. Seneca lays so much stress upon her unworthy passion for

markable influence of Seneca upon the Elizabethan drama in general, it would not be at all surprising if his influence extended to the shaping of the villain-hero type in particular.

Seneca follows Euripides in making Medea a villain as well as the heroine, but in the process he transforms her into a monster. In the first part of the Greek play, all our sympathy is awakened for Medea. We despise Jason. It is not until the heroine contemplates revenge that our sympathy is in the least abated. We could almost forgive her for an open murder of her enemies. When she contemplates the murder of her children, however, she begins to appear monstrous ; but this feeling again merges into pity when we see how she suffers at the thought of losing them. Moreover, Euripides seeks to lessen the horror of the deed by laying stress upon the fact that Medea is killing her children to keep them from being killed by her enemies. But when she actually murders them, and triumphs in the car above Jason's head, rejoicing in her victory over him, and showing no signs of mother-pity, our aversion once more masters us. Nevertheless, the feeling that we carry away from a perusal of the play is one of mingled pity and aversion in which the former is fully as powerful as the latter.

In Seneca's tragedy the effect is quite different. Medea herself opens the play with a blood-curdling

---

Ægisthus that Agamemnon's previous treatment of Iphigenia, and the fact that he belongs to a doomed house, almost disappear in the background. It is only the fact that Agamemnon looms up so large in Greek history that saves this tragedy from being classed with *Thyestes* and *Medea*.

soliloquy, calling upon the powers above and below
to damn for ever Jason, Creon, and Creüsa :

. . . and ye

Whose aid Medea may more boldly claim, thou world
Of endless night, th' antipodes of heavenly realms,
Ye damned ghosts, thou lord of hades' dark domain,   10
Whose mistress was with trustier pledge won to thy side—
Before ye all this baleful prayer I bring : Be near !
Be near ! Ye crime-avenging furies, come and loose
Your horrid locks with serpent coils entwined, and grasp
With bloody hands the smoking torch ; be near as once 15
Ye stood in dread array beside my wedding couch.
Upon this new-made bride destruction send, and death
Upon the king and all the royal line ! But he,
My husband, may he live to meet some heavier doom ;
This curse I imprecate upon his head ; . . .[1]

This dire curse at once alienates sympathy. We
get the impression that Medea is an evil woman,
and this impression becomes fixed, for the act is
closed by the chorus immediately following this
soliloquy. Medea does not tell of her own wrongs
until Act II ; and when she there enumerates the
crimes she has been guilty of for Jason's sake, the
cruelty of the deeds swallows up the reason for
them. In Act III, in a conference with Jason, she
learns that he loves his children, but she only makes
use of this discovery to inflict brutal punishment.
In Euripides, her children are to be banished, and
she seeks to have them protected. In Seneca, the
children are safe in the father's hands, which makes
her slaughter of them the more revolting. In the
fourth act she appears chanting horrible incantations,[2]
and herself steeps the bridal gifts in the brew that
is to make them fatal. Finally, in the fifth act, she

---

[1] Miller's translation.
[2] Note the medieval element in the magic and black arts.

slays her children before the audience, and exults
in the suffering of Jason. Her own hesitation over
killing the children is scarcely touched as a motive.
The result is that she becomes an extremely unsympathetic protagonist.   The effect of the combination of villain and protagonist is disappointing ;
the emotions called forth are as untragic as Aristotle
predicted.

In the tragedy of *Thyestes* the murderer Atreus
appears as the villain. The mere fact that he is a
murderer, however, does not make him a villain. We
must remember that the wilfulness of the act is as
important as the act itself. With the exception of
Medea, none of the classical criminals seems to be
acting altogether voluntarily.   Thyestes suffers
because he is the son of a doomed house ; and even
Atreus is inspired by the Ghost of Tantalus, who in
turn is driven on by the Fury to do his allotted part.
But in the case of Atreus this motive is lost sight of
in his horrible cruelty and exultation in torture.
He is one of the most monstrous creations in
dramatic literature. As he prepares his brother's
children as a feast for the parent, and glories in his
wickedness, he is actually loathsome. With him
we may fairly say it is crime for crime's sake.

> *Atreus.*   . . . 'Tis sweet to note
> The father's frantic grief when first he sees
> His children's gory heads ; to catch his words,
> To watch his colour change ; to see him sit,
> All breathless with the shock, in dumb amaze,
> In frozen horror at the gruesome sight.   905
> This is the sweet reward of all my toil—
> To see his misery, e'en as it grows
> Upon his soul.[1]

> [1] Act V, Miller's translation.

Atreus is, in fact, the paragon of villains ; the question is whether he is also the hero. The play is named after Thyestes, and, according to the Greek conception of the gods punishing evil from generation to generation until the original sin had been balanced by the punishment, the fate Thyestes meets with in this tragedy for the sins of his ancestors would doubtless have made him the protagonist in the estimation of a Greek audience. For Thyestes and Atreus were the sons of Pelops who was served as a dish to the gods by his father Tantalus ; and from Atreus sprang Agamemnon who was killed by his wife. This whole family was so submerged in crime, and was so well known to the Greeks, that the tragic end of any one of them would have made that one the protagonist in their eyes. It is to be said also for Seneca's tragedy that the audience is informed by narration of the evil deeds committed in the past by Thyestes against his brother. But Thyestes is repentant, and has already suffered for his past sins by poverty and banishment when he is introduced to us. Consequently we are inclined to sympathize with him. When Tantalus and the Fury have retired after a prologue called Act I, Atreus appears in soliloquy and at once becomes the centre of interest. We hope that his scheme to entice his brother back will not be successful ; we are most interested in him from beginning to end, because we wish him to fail in everything which he attempts ; we are so filled with loathing and hatred for him that we have little or no feeling, not even of pity, left for anyone else. It is not the effect of his machinations upon Thyestes

as a hero with whom we are in sympathy that is
the centre of interest, but his own frightful crimes,
his colossal wickedness, his conflict with moral
law.   Moreover, he has the chief acting part and
speaks the greatest number of lines, so that he may
reasonably be classed as the hero according to our
definition.

Unless the Elizabethans were thoroughly familiar
with Greek legendary history and the Greek idea of
retribution, as well as with the classic method of
presenting merely the culmination of an action,
they must have been much impressed by the pre-
ponderating part played by the criminals.   Consider for a moment the startling nature of the
Senecan themes :

Œdipus is guilty of incest, and gouges out his
own eyes ;   Clytemnestra commits adultery, and
murders her husband ;   Medea slaughters her own
children, and hurls them down to her husband from
the housetop ;   Atreus makes his brother drunk at a
banquet, and serves him the flesh of his own children !

Considered in the bald outline, could any facts
be more gruesome ?   And yet these plays were
constantly read by the Elizabethan poets, and were
regarded as the best examples of dramatic art.
Violence and murder were before them as model
themes for imitation, and in at least two of Seneca's
plays the protagonists were themselves villains.
Having the sanction of classicism, and appealing
to the imagination of that era, these tragedies undoubtedly exercised some influence in directing the
Elizabethan playwright's choice and handling of

theme, so that Seneca, if he did not furnish the
actual models, may be said at least to have suggested
the plot with the villain as hero.

The Elizabethans, however, must be credited
with one distinct advance. The tragedy of *Thyestes*
does not end unhappily for Atreus : he is successful
in his designs and suffers no punishment. The same
is true of Medea. Of course, the fact that the plays
open only with the last phase of an action, and that
those who do meet with misfortune are suffering
because of their own past or the deeds of their
ancestors, and likewise the fact that he who triumphs
now will suffer in the play to follow, makes it
excusable for the villain to succeed ; but the
effect, nevertheless, upon the reader at the close of
one of these tragedies is anything but pleasing ; it
is distressing. Successful villainy adds shock to
the horror of the crimes. If these plays served in
any way as models for the Elizabethans, the reversal of fortune at the end for the villain-hero was
their own addition. In presenting the whole of an
action, though they were not squeamish in the
actions they imitated, they recognized that a spectator demands at least some satisfaction for his moral
sense if he cannot be elevated, and they consequently saw to it that the villain perished for his
crimes before the curtain fell, though they had to
strain a point to kill him.

III

ENGLISH PLAYS BEFORE MARLOWE

BETWEEN 1587 and 1616 many plays containing Senecan characteristics were produced. Whether, however, those characteristics were the result of direct contact with Seneca's tragedies only, or the result not only of contact with Seneca, but also with earlier English Senecan plays written between 1561-2 and 1587—between the dates of *Gorboduc* and *Tamburlaine*—is a question almost impossible to determine. Of such plays, *Gorboduc, Tancred and Gismunda, Jocasta,* and *The Misfortunes of Arthur* are distinctly Senecan. Taken with *Damon and Pithias, Appius and Virginia, Horestes, Cambyses,* and *Promus and Cassandra*—all of which show comparatively little Senecan influence—they comprehend all the extant English tragedies before 1587. *Jocasta, Damon and Pithias,* and *Horestes* may be dismissed without further notice, as being obviously outside the class of plays in which the villain plays the rôle of protagonist. The remaining purely Senecan plays will likewise be found to contain no such hero. Only *Appius and Virginia, Cambyses,* and *Promus and Cassandra* may have exerted some influence in shaping that particular character-type.

Gorboduc, or *Ferrex and Porrex*, the first of many plays representing the fall of English kings after classical models, deals chiefly, in long speeches, with political morality, laying stress on the evils of a divided kingdom. The father partitions the realm between his two sons, of whom the elder is the favourite of the mother. The sons, misled and egged on by evil counsellors, wage war against each other. The younger kills the elder, and is in turn murdered by the mother, after which both father and mother are killed by the mob, and the kingdom long disordered. All the evils are set in motion by the folly—but not the criminality—of the father. Neither of the sons can be called a villain, as each is misinformed by courtiers as to the conduct and intentions of the other, and neither is conscious that he is doing anything criminal or even wrongful. Only the mother, who acts consciously and from revenge, falls within our definition of a villain. She, however, is not the protagonist.

Tancred and Gismunda was acted in 1568 under the title of *Gismond of Salerne*. The play received the title of *Tancred and Gismunda* when it was revised and rewritten in 1591 by Robert Wilmot, the author of the original fifth act. The cruel incidents in the tragedy may have increased the effect produced upon later dramatists by similar incidents in Seneca, but the play itself cannot be reckoned as a forerunner of the villain-hero type. Tancred is selfish, jealous, tyrannical, and cruel when enraged ; but villain as he is, he is so feebly characterized, and his speeches are so artificial, that his actions arouse very little emotion. Moreover,

Gismunda, not Tancred, is the protagonist. The play was correctly named in the first place—*Gismond of Salerne*. Tancred, it is true, suffers a tragical end as the result of his cruelty, but he is not the figure of chief interest ; the lovers hold that position. It is primarily the story of Gismunda, who, giving way to her passions and defying her father's wishes, suffers to extremity as the result. If Gismunda were more subtly characterized this would be more evident.

The Misfortunes of Arthur bears some resemblance to Seneca's *Agamemnon*, and like it suggests the villain-hero type of play because the villain is before us so frequently. Our sympathies, however, are all with Arthur, and the leading motive of the tragedy—the visitation upon the children of the sins of the father (Pendragon)—demands that we rank him as hero.

Appius and Virginia (by R. B.) was printed in 1575, and perhaps acted[1] some time between 1563 and 1567. The play opens with a scene of domestic bliss in the family of Virginius. After our sympathies are aroused, Appius is introduced with considerable dramatic contrast plotting the seduction of Virginia. This is only prevented by the courage of Virginia who, rather than suffer shame, allows her father to cut off her head. Appius, in turn, is executed through the intervention of the abstractions Justice and Reward.

The play was undoubtedly written to celebrate virtue. As a simple story it would teach that fame

[1] Cf. Schelling, *Elizabethan Drama*, Vol. I, p. 120, citing Fleay, i, 27 ; " Stage," 61.

lives after death, and that he who dies for virtue really conquers. But neither of the virtuous characters is the hero of the tragedy. Appius, the villain, plays that rôle. The death of Virginia is in no way the result of tragic guilt ; she and her father are merely acted upon and driven to the fatal sacrifice, not through any fault of their own, but to escape a greater evil. The criminal lust of Appius is the motive power of the whole action. *Appius and Virginia* stands, therefore, as one of the early examples of a villain-hero play. But it can hardly be said that the author consciously strove to produce such a drama, for, with the exception of a couple of lines in the opening speech of Appius regretting his fall from virtue, the characterization is spent on Virginius and Virginia. Consequently, the hero simply excites aversion. Moreover, the presence of many allegorical figures in the play renders it half Morality, and deprives it of any considerable dramatic effectiveness. The intrusion of Justice and Reward interferes with the natural flow of our emotions. Instead of being permitted to enjoy to what extent we may the emotions proper to tragedy, we have foisted upon us poetic justice in its most artificial and unconvincing form. A sermon is substituted for a tragedy.

Cambyses was written about 1569–70 by Thomas Preston. The plot is set forth on the title page with full emphasis on the various motives : " A Lamentable Tragedie mixed full of pleasant mirth containing the life of Cambises King of Persia from the beginning of his kingdome unto his Death, his one good deede of execution, after that many

wicked deedes and tyrannous murders committed
by and through him, and last of all, his odious
death by Gods Justice appointed." His one good
deed is the execution of an unjust judge who has
been abusing his power during Cambyses' absence.
After that he proceeds to shoot his minister's son, to
prove that wine has not affected his nerves ; next
he murders his brother ; then his bride ; but is
finally killed by his own sword flying out of its
scabbard and sticking in his side.

There is scarcely any motive whatever for Cambyses' conduct ; his career is simply a series of
murders. There are so many characters of the
morality plays worked into the plot that if Cambyses himself were named Tyranny, or Wicked
Deeds, the play might pass for an example of that
type of drama. As it is, the character of Everyman,
in the Morality of that name, is much more lifelike
than that of the historical hero of this " Lamentable
Tragedie." Seneca is referred to in the prologue,
but aside from the figure of the cruel tyrant, there
are very few Senecan characteristics noticeable. If
the play was at all successful it must have been
owing purely to the sensationalism of the disconnected scenes, or to the morality elements.

Weak as the play is, however, it may have had
some influence upon later dramatists. For Cambyses, the king, though poorly psychologized, is at
once a villain and the hero. He is the protagonist
in the strictest sense of the word, for the tragedy is
not intended to illustrate the effect of his machinations on anyone else, but solely to present his own
evil deeds. The play must, therefore, be listed as

one of the two or three of this type which Marlowe may have considered before creating his villain-hero.

Promus and Cassandra (1578), by George Whetstone, is important both as the source of *Measure for Measure* and as a forerunner of the type we have under discussion.   In the first half of the play Promus is certainly the protagonist.   It is he who has sentenced Andrugio to death ; it is the workings of his mind, his struggle between duty and desire, that is most strongly presented to us after he has had his interview with Cassandra ;   it is he who forces upon Cassandra her choice between dishonour and her brother's death ;   and finally it is he who breaks his promise and orders Andrugio to be put to death.   As these incidents constitute practically the entire action of Part I, Promus is clearly the central figure.   The mere enumeration of the above motives, however, makes it equally clear that his conduct is villainous.   Nevertheless, Promus is not represented as conscienceless.   He has the reputation of a just man, and he recognizes the injustice of his demands ;   but lust forces him to yield to his animal nature.   After the deed is done there is a struggle in his mind as to whether he shall live up to his promise or not.   He realizes the double wickedness of executing Andrugio and refusing to marry Cassandra, but he fears scandal and so plays the villain.

By endeavouring to portray the struggle in the mind of Promus, the author hit upon the one motive which might have made his villain a sympathetic hero.   For when a man earnestly

struggles against the evil in his own nature we
nearly always sympathize with him, and interest
ourselves in his ultimate fortunes. It is very
doubtful, however, whether an audience could
ever be won over by a man whose ruling passion
was lust ; for lust is essentially base, and though
crimes involving great ability may attract us
towards the criminal, vice and petty crimes repel.
At any rate, Whetstone was unequal to the task
before him. Having touched upon what was vital
in his tragedy in Part I, he abandoned it in
Part II. It was during the absence of the king
that Promus committed the crimes which forced
him into prominence. In the second half of the play
the king returns, and at once assumes the chief
acting part. He instigates an inquiry, the outcome
of which is so certain that we simply await his final
separation of the sheep from the goats. Promus, as
an actor, sinks into the background, and his position becomes almost as unimportant as Andrugio's
rôle in Part I. Neither the fear, the remorse, nor
the defiance that, in a thoughtful character study,
we might expect to govern Promus as the result of
the approaching exposure of his past actions, is
elaborated. When he is accused before the king by
Cassandra he admits his guilt as though, indeed,
he were affected by remorse, and when he is being
led to apparent death he shows some courage ;
but these motives are not managed in such a way
as to cause his actions to appear inevitable. A
lighter note is struck in the second play ; comedy
is uppermost ; and Promus as a tragic figure is
forgotten.

The difference in tone between the two parts of
the drama is analogous to the imperfect blending of
elements in each part taken separately. The effectiveness of the play is greatly marred by its length
and lack of unity, but chiefly by the very means
through which its author sought to lend it distinction, viz. by the observance of " decorum." In the
division of the play into five acts, in the moral
sentiments, and in the soliloquies, Whetstone manifests an intention of treating his subject seriously
in the classic manner ; but along with his serious
treatment he mingles the " pleasant mirth " of the
morality in such a fashion as to bring about a most
confusing mixture of tragedy, comedy, and farce.
The farcical elements so affect the whole that the
tragic impression is totally destroyed.

Although the play fails to stimulate deep emotion, for the reasons above stated, it undoubtedly
influenced later dramatists. In the first place we
know that in *Measure for Measure*[1] Shakespeare
takes over practically the whole story, simply re-
modelling it to make it more effective. He repro-
duces such motives of the old play as the absent
duke, the unfortunate brother, and the unhappy
sister abused by the unworthy deputy. The deputy
Angelo, is again both hero and villain, but his conduct is much more impressive than that of Promus,
owing to thoughtful character study. It is note-
worthy, however, that of the dramatists more concerned with the relation of action to character,
than with intrigues and dramatic situations divorced
from character, Shakespeare and Webster alone

[1] See Appendix.

undertook to present as their hero a villain actuated solely by lust. In so doing both borrowed old stories already staged before 1580.[1] Shakespeare with all his genius seems to have felt, however, that the motive of lust could not be transformed into elevating tragedy, for he turns *Measure for Measure* into a comedy.[2] On the other hand, the tragedies, or tragi-comedies, of Beaumont and Fletcher introduce numerous lustful characters upon whose actions the plot depends. Without making a special study, however, one could hardly say just what the effect was of *Promus and Cassandra* upon this school.

It is evident, if the foregoing review is fair, that Marlowe was not an actual innovator in adapting the tragic villain to the position of protagonist. He not only had the example of Seneca before him, but, among English plays of the popular sort, *Cambyses*, *Appius and Virginia*, and *Promus and Cassandra*. Yet these latter plays do not seem to have exerted any specific influence upon the dramatists of the latter part of the sixteenth century. If they noticed that the villain was also protagonist, the inferior quality of the tragedies offered no incentive to produce more dramas of the same type. Certainly the villainy of the later heroes is of a different character from that of the villains we have just discussed. Concerning Seneca's influence, however, more may be said. Marlowe and his fellow-dramatists probably felt themselves strongly supported by the authority of Seneca once they decided to

[1] See Webster's *Appius and Virginia* in Appendix.
[2] See Appendix.

develop the villain-hero type. But a far more definite influence than even that of Seneca was affecting Marlowe ; an influence that accounts specifically, not for the villain as hero, but for the type of villain chosen as hero. As if to assist the dramatist in baring the motives that underlay the conduct of powerful and faithless princes, there aptly appeared certain works of and about Machiavelli, in which the principles of villainy were so carefully outlined that wickedness in high places was thereafter as explicable as goodness itself.

IV

MACHIAVELLI [1]

THE PRINCE, which contains the gist of Machia-velli's political doctrine, was written in 1513, but was not published until 1532, five years after the author's death. In the meantime it was extensively circulated in manuscript, but was certainly not considered scandalous or detrimental to the Church, for its publication was decreed in 1531 by Clement VII.[2] Two editions of *The Prince* appeared within a year. Very soon afterwards the denunciations commenced and continued with growing warmth until 1559, when Machiavelli's works were put on

[1] Machiavelli, the Florentine statesman and philosopher, was born in 1469 and died just thirty-six years before Marlowe was born. His life thus appears to have been contemporaneous with the reigns of Richard III, Henry VII, and Henry VIII of England ; Charles VIII, Louis XII, and Francis I of France ; the Emperor Charles V of Germany ; and with the ecclesiastical and political domination of the Borgias and Medici in Italy. He made a study of the lives and principles of these princes, as well as of the rulers of antiquity, and his political opinions, based upon his study of these men, were circulated in book form as *The Prince* and the *Discourses*.

[2] Papal bull in Amico : La Vita di Nic. Mach. 1876, p. 415. For a history of Machiavelli's writings and their effect upon public opinion in Europe, cf. Mohl, *Die Geschichte und Literatur der Staatswissenschaften ;* Janet, *Histoire de la science politique dans ses rapports avec la morale ;* Burd, *Il Principe ;* Meyer, *Machiavelli and the Elizabethan Drama ;* Villari, *Life and Times of Machiavelli ;* from which most of the statements concerning Machiavelli in the following pages are drawn.

the Index by Paul IV. As the books continued to
circulate, however, criticism became even more
vehement, until it reached its height while Marlowe
was in college. The author was regarded as the
fiend incarnate. The terms used to describe him
" would seem," says Macaulay,[1] " to import that
he was the tempter, the evil principle, the discoverer
of ambition and revenge, the original inventor of
perjury, and that, before the publication of his fatal
Prince, there had never been a hypocrite, a tyrant, or
a traitor, a simulated virtue, or a convenient crime."

That such a series of violent denunciations should
follow so soon upon the publication of *The Prince*,
which, though well known for twenty years immediately preceding, had aroused practically no
comment ; and that one pope should issue a bull
against the works which had been published just a
quarter of a century before by the decree of his
predecessor, seems most extraordinary. Villari
explains the change of attitude on the ground that
in the interim the Medici, who in Machiavelli's time
were little more than protectors of the republic of
Florence, had become oppressive tyrants after his
death ; and that religious feeling, long dormant
while the Church at Rome was fighting for tem-
poral power in jealous rivalry with the Italian
states, had been awakened by the Reformation in
Germany. Machiavelli had accused the Catholic
Church of being the ruin of Italy. This charge,
which fell on deaf ears at the time, could no longer
be submitted to with indifference by the men who
were endeavouring to restore her authority. On

[1] *Critical and Historical Essays*, Vol. I.

the other hand, Machiavelli's apparent indifference
to the claims of conscience aroused the hostility of
the Protestants. Consequently he was subjected
to a cross-fire from all their guns. The fact that his
works were much admired by statesmen of high
renown, but of unscrupulous conduct, and that their
actions seemed to fit in perfectly with the principles
set forth in *The Prince,* led many to suppose that
The Prince was the source of all the corruption and
high-handed methods then practised.

The French Huguenots, avowed enemies of
despotism, were the most severe in their attacks.
Gentillet,[1] in particular, by an unfair but sensational
selection of maxims, increased the feeling of colossal
wickedness with which the name of Machiavelli
was associated. His book, popularly known as
Anti-Machiavel, was published just four years after
the massacre of St. Bartholomew's Day, and in it
Gentillet attributes that outrage to the influence
of Machiavelli's doctrines. He accuses the Florentine of atheism, ignorance, cruelty, tyranny, usury,
and of every detestable vice, and claims that his
followers in France are avaricious, and that they
are amassing great wealth by extortion. Fearing
that Machiavelli's teachings may prove the ruin of
France, he offers his own book as an "antidote to
the poison." It is to this book that Burd[2] ascribes
the rise of so-called " Machiavellism."

[1] *Discours sur les Moyens de bien gouverner et maintenir en
bonne paix un Royaume ou autre Principauté : Divisez en trois
Parties : a savoir, du Conseil, de la Religion et Policie que doit
tenir un Prince : Contre Nicholas Machiavel, Florentin. A
Treshaut et Tres-illustre Prince François Duc d'Alençon fils et
frere de Roy,* 1576.

[2] Supra.

Gentillet divides his book into three parts, treating of the counsel, religion, and policy which a prince ought to have. Under each heading he groups a certain number of maxims selected from different parts of the *Discourses* and *The Prince*. After stating the maxims, he branches out into lengthy essays wherein he exhausts the literature of antiquity to refute them. Such a method, though unjust because it omitted the context, was remarkably effective in centring attention on Machiavelli's most striking axioms. The book at once attracted universal attention, and was almost immediately (1577) translated into English by Simon Patericke. The most important of these maxims, which contain the essence of that Machiavellism which haunted the Elizabethan stage, are as follows : [1]

I

1. A Prince's good Counsell ought to proceed from his owne wisedome, otherwise, he cannot be well counselled.

II

1. A Prince above all things ought to wish and desire to be esteemed Devout, although hee be not so indeed.

2. A Prince ought to sustaine and confirme that which is false in Religion, if so be it turne to the favour thereof.

III

4. A Prince in a country newly conquered, must subvert & destroy all such as suffer great losse in that conquest,

[1] In the Appendix Gentillet's maxims are printed in full, just as they appeared in the 1608 edition of Simon Patericke's translation, which is an exact reproduction of Gentillet, except for the dedication to Francis Hastings and Edward Bacon. Patericke's translation is entitled, *A Discourse upon the Means of Well Governing and Maintaining in Good Peace a Kingdome, or Other Principality*. It was printed in London by Adam Islip, 1608.

and altogether root out the blood and race of such as before governed there.

6. It is folly to thinke, with Princes and great Lords, that new pleasures will cause them to forget old offences.

7. A Prince ought to propound unto himselfe to imitate Cæsar Borgia, the sonne of Pope Alexander the sixt.

8. A Prince need not care to be accounted cruell, if so be that he can make himselfe to be obeyed thereby.

9. It is better for a Prince to be feared than loved.

10. A Prince ought not to trust in the amitie of men.

12. A Prince ought to follow the nature of the Lyon and of the Foxe, yet not of the one without the other.

14. A Prince ought to exercise cruelty all at once ; and to do pleasures by little & little.

18. A Prince ought not to feare to be periured, to deceive, and dissemble ; for the deceiver alwaies finds some that are fit to be deceived.

20. A Prince, which (as it were constrained) useth Clemencie and Lenitie, advanceth his owne destruction.

22. Faith, Clemencie, and Liberalitie, are vertues very damageable to a Prince : but it is good, that of them he only have some similitude and likenesse.

23. A Prince ought to have a turning and winding wit, with art and practise made fit to bee cruell & unfaithfull, that he may shew himselfe such an one when there is need.

26. Illiberalitie is commendable in a Prince, and the reputation of a handycraftsman, is a dishonour without evill will.

27. A Prince which will make a straight profession of a good man, cannot long continue in the world amongst such an heape of naughtie and wicked people.

31. Civile seditions and dissensions are profitable, and not to be blamed.

33. A Prince which feareth his subiects, ought to build fortresses in his country, to hold them in obedience.

34. A Prince ought to commit to another those affaires which are subiect to hatred & envy, and reserve to himselfe such as depend upon his grace and favour.

The presentations of the maxims in this handy form, together with the fierce denunciations accompanying them, had an immediate effect upon

English readers.[1] Until the appearance of Gentillet
and Patericke, references in English literature to
Machiavelli were comparatively few, and showed no
disposition on the part of the authors to misinter-
pret his principles. But from that time on, scarcely
a year was allowed to pass without references,
either to the statesman or to his " policy," which
showed a growing inclination to treat him as the
fiend represented by Gentillet.

In 1578, the year following Patericke's translation, there appeared a Latin work by Gabriel Harvey[2]
one poem of which was certainly inspired by
the Gentillet–Patericke diatribes. The poem[3] is
headed :

Epigramma in Effigiem Machiavelli
Machiavellus ipse loquitur

Machiavelli, speaking in person, says in sub-
stance :

> Let no one think to govern who does not know my rules,
> nor think he has gained wisdom who does not know them
> well. My talk is only of kingdoms and sceptres, of camps
> and wars. In my hand I bear a sword and my tongue is
> sprinkled with a thousand poisons. My motto is and always
> has been : " Ambition ; either Cæsar or nothing." Milk
> is food for babes, I feed on blood. Blood is nothing, torture
> is nothing : let lowly minds perish. I alone have wisdom,
> I live, and triumph by myself. Fraud is my greatest
> virtue ; the next is force. I know no other gods.

[1] " Machiavelli and the Elizabethan Drama," by Edward
Meyer, published in *Litterarhistorische Forschungen*, Vol. I (1897).
I am much indebted to Dr. Meyer for what I have to offer on
Machiavelli and the drama.

[2] ΧΑΙΡΕ vel Gabrielis Harveij Gratulationum Valdensium
Libri quattuor, London, 1578.

[3] The poem is printed in full in Meyer, p. 22.

As Meyer says, " This is simply Gentillet epito-
mized ; here we have the four principal crimes
ascribed to Machiavelli later on in the drama :
poison, murder, fraud, and violence. Especially
is poison to be noted ; for the Florentine himself
nowhere expressly recommends its use. It became,
however, the prime factor in Elizabethan Machiavellism." The nonchalant way in which blood and
torture are referred to by the Machiavelli of the
poem might lead one familiar with Elizabethan
drama to think the lines had been written after the
appearance of Barabas, Aaron, and Eleazor, instead of years before. But more important than
the words of the speaker is the heading *Machiavellus
ipse loquitur*, because of the strong suggestion it
carries that Marlowe had this poem before him when
he made Machiavelli himself speak the prologue to
The Jew of Malta.

Another matter of significance in estimating the
influence of Machiavelli is the rapidity with which
his works came into favour at Cambridge. In 1579
Harvey claimed that his works had supplanted all
others, and hinted at the harm they were doing
among individuals.[1] Greene was a student at
Cambridge at this time, and Marlowe the year following. By 1583 we find that Machiavelli's name
was so well known that Greene felt safe in making
an abstract noun of it in *Mamillia*. The characteristics which he considers Machiavellian are entirely
in accord with Gentillet's representations : " So
Pharicles . . . being in the state of his life such a

[1] Cf. Meyer, p. 25, quoting letter from "Letter-book" ed.
Scott, p. 79.

mutable Machavilian, as he neither regarded friend nor faith, oath nor promise, if his wavering wit perswaded him to the contrary." [1]

But of still greater importance in connection with our study is a book called *Leycester's Common-wealth*, attributed to Father Parsons,[2] which came out in 1584. It is important because it was widely read, and because it contains three Machiavellian maxims which Leicester was accused of acting upon, and which appear time and again in the later drama. They are as follows :

1. That Princes being unable to give sufficient satisfaction for the benefit of being helped to a crown should recompense such friends with death.[3]

2. That Princes should drive such as they desire to get rid of to " attempt somewhat whereby they may incur danger, or remain in perpetual suspition or disgrace." [4]

3. " Where you have once done a great injury, there you must never forgive." [5]

The effect that Machiavelli's writings were having all over Europe in agitating questions concerning political policy, Biblical doctrine, and private conscience was not lost upon the dramatists. When the principles of conduct of such men as Richard III and Cæsar Borgia were reduced to a system and presented in axiomatic form ; and when

---

[1] *Mamillia*, ed. Grosart, II, 205. Cf. Meyer, p. 27.
[2] Cf. Meyer, p. 28 and note 4.
[3] Leys. Com. (1641), 92. Cf. *The Prince*, III ; *Discourses*, II, 33 (265) ; *Ist. Fior.*, IV (253).
[4] *Ibid.*, 149. Cf. *The Prince*, VII ; Gentillet, III, 11.
[5] *Ibid.*, 177. Cf. *The Prince*, VII ; *Discourses*, III, 4 (312); *Ist. Fior.*, IV, (217) ; Gentillet, III, 6.

examples of such conduct in high places, as, for
instance, the treatment accorded by Henry VIII
to Wolsey and Cromwell, were still fresh in men's
minds ; they exercised a great fascination over the
dramatic artist. Nothing could be more natural,
for such principles not only suggested the interesting situations arising where the will and the conscience of man conflict, but tempted the dramatist
to illustrate and magnify the force of character
produced by the cultivation of mere " virtù." [1]
The first of the dramatists to feel this fascination,
and the first to bring Machiavelli on the stage was
Marlowe. Having within himself a passionate
admiration for " virtù," having before him in axiomatic form the principles of conduct that should
guide a man influenced more by will than conscience,
foreseeing the dramatic possibilities of such a character, favoured by a public not unfamiliar with the
tyrant as hero, he seized upon the opportunity
which offered itself, made his hero a Machiavellian,
touched the drama with the magic wand of poetry,
and presented *The Jew of Malta*.

[1] Cf. Courthope, Vol. II, p. 28.

V

MARLOWE AND THE MACHIAVELLIAN VILLAIN-HERO

In establishing the villain-hero type which dominated the stage in the last decade of the sixteenth
century we are forced back upon the character of
Lorenzo of *The Spanish Tragedy*. Lorenzo certainly cannot be considered the hero, but he is
important because as a villain he is the prototype
of Barabas. Though much indebted to Seneca, the
author of *The Spanish Tragedy* is likewise indebted
to Machiavelli. The revenge of a father for a son
is the leading motive, and this puts Hieronimo in
the technical position of hero. The psychological
treatment of his grief and his madness, taken with
his plot of revenge, makes him the central figure.
But Lorenzo plays a close second. He is much more
active and important in shaping the action than is
Claudius in *Hamlet*. In *Hamlet* the crime that calls
for revenge has already been committed ; consequently we are free to centre our attention upon
the effect of the knowledge of the deed upon Hamlet
himself. But in *The Spanish Tragedy* the murder
which stimulates Hieronimo's revenge is committed
by Lorenzo before our very eyes ; accordingly the
murderer becomes more prominent in the same

relative position than in *Hamlet*. In the second place, Lorenzo continues to be very active in placing his sister in confinement, in blocking Hieronimo, and in disposing of his accomplices.

Now, the importance of Lorenzo's activity from our point of view is that it is the result of Machiavellian "policy." He is not, indeed, represented as a man of boundless ambition, nor is he a prince ✓ relying upon the doctrines of Machiavelli to govern his state ; but in his indifference to the welfare of others, as in the means he takes to attain his own ends, he might serve as the perfect pattern of the Machiavellian courtiers inveighed against by Patericke and Gentillet.[1] In the first place, he is an egotist, and egotism is one of the distinguishing features of Machiavellians. The line

I'll trust myself, myself shall be my friend,   (*Sp. Tr.*, III)

to which he gives utterance, is born of the same belief in self that later leads Barabas to say

Ego mihimet sum semper proximus,

and closely resembles an expression used by Richard III :

I am myself alone.

He uses men like wedges to drive out one another, and puts his accomplices to death.[2] This is not done on the spur of the moment, but is part of a

---

[1] See Dedication and Preface to Patericke's translation of Gentillet.

[2] Lorenzo uses Serberine in the murder of Horatio, bribes Pedringano to shoot Serberine, and has Pedringano hung for the deed before he can betray the part played by Lorenzo.

carefully considered policy resulting from his egotism, as he confides to the audience :

> Thus must we work, that will avoid distrust,
> Thus must we practice to avoid mishap :
> And thus one ill another must expulse.
>
> And better 'tis that base companions die,
> Than by their life to hazard our good haps :
> Nor shall they live for me to fear their fate ;
> I'll trust myself, myself shall be my friend ;
> For die they shall, slaves are ordained to no other end.
>
> (*Sp. Tr.*, III.)

This ridding one's self of accomplices is the very essence of Machiavellism. It was the practice of Cæsar Borgia, and is discussed in *The Prince*, Chapter VIII. Barabas adopted the same policy, and it became a characteristic of Machiavellian villains.

The sentiment expressed in the two lines above quoted, beginning " And better 'tis," is easily recognizable when it again crops out in Barabas :

> For so I live, perish may all the world !   (V, 177.)

The idea expressed in the line

> And thus one ill another must expulse,

although quite in accord with the conclusions to be drawn from Machiavelli's maxims, is probably of Senecan origin, for it is reproduced in Latin in another part of the same play in almost identically the same form found in Seneca's *Agamemnon :*

> Per scelus semper tutum est sceleribus iter.   (*Sp. Tr.*)
> Per scelera semper sceleribus tutum est iter. (*Agam.*, 116.)

The fact that Senecan lines are frequently in the mouths of Machiavellians is easily explained, for

these villains model their lives upon the immoral
maxims which Seneca simply expresses in order to
refute. Machiavelli himself seems sometimes to
have put most faith in the side of the argument
which the Roman philosopher regarded as sophisti-
cal. Machiavelli's traducers, at any rate, put him
in a class as a teacher with Seneca's tyrants.

One other passage in *The Spanish Tragedy* is
strongly reminiscent of Machiavelli :

> Where words prevail not, violence prevails,
> But gold doth more than either of them both. (*Sp. Tr.*, II.)

This both reflects the policy of those tyrants mentioned by Machiavelli who attempt to establish
themselves by bribery, and suggests the maxim
(III, 12), quoted by Gentillet, that " A Prince ought
to follow the nature of the Lyon and of the Foxe, yet
not of the one without the other."

The general atmosphere of violence and death
in this play, and the summary of all the horrors
by the Ghost at the end of the action, are Senecan.
But, as we have seen, the manner in which Lorenzo
contributes to the action is Machiavellian. Had he
been trying to elevate himself, instead of simply
seeking revenge in the interest of his friend Beltha-
zar,[1] he might have advanced to the first place in
the drama and become a Machiavellian hero. As it
is, we find in his nature the following typical
characteristics : he is egotistical, guileful, cruel,
faithless, remorseless, and murderous. He also
removes accomplices. Without playing the leading
part, he leads a tragic career which somewhat

---

[1] He may have been trying to advance his house by an alliance
with the Portuguese prince, but this motive is not emphasized.

resembles that of Barabas. He begins his tragic
career from hatred, pursues his purpose by craft,
underestimates the ability of his adversary, is
betrayed by an accomplice, and finally succumbs
to the craft of others.

The Jew of Malta is so well known, and general
and obvious criticism has been so comprehensively
stated by Bullen,[1] Ward,[2] and others, that any
prefatory remarks to our special study scarcely
seem necessary. Hallam is quite in accord with
universal opinion in saying that the first two acts
"are more vigorously conceived, both as to character and to circumstance, than any other Elizabethan play except those of Shakespeare." Barabas'
passion for gold, which is rivalled only by his love
for his daughter, is of such gigantic proportions
that it leaves upon our minds an impression of
magnificent ambition which even the degeneration
of the play in the last three acts, and the exhibition
of Barabas as a monstrous stage villain, fail totally
to eradicate.

How many of the motives of special scenes were
taken over from the direct source, it is impossible
to say, the specific historical documents from which
Marlowe probably drew the story being unknown ;
but the gruesome horror of the play was in accord,
at any rate, with the spirit of the age in which it
was produced. The general influence of Seneca
is likewise apparent. The characteristics which
Cunliffe enumerates as Senecan are all to be found
in *The Jew of Malta :* Sensationalism, including

---

[1] *Works of Marlowe*, I, p. xl–xliii.
[2] *Hist. Eng. Dram. Lit.*, I, 337 ff.

horror of incident and exaggeration of expression,
Rhetoric, Fatalism, Contempt of Death, and
Soliloquy. Even the use of poison is not unknown
in Seneca, although never there employed in
Barabas' wholesale manner.[1] Indeed, though
Seneca is to be reckoned with, he can be said to
have exerted only a general influence over this
tragedy ; Machiavelli was its real inspiration.
Marlowe has not, however, confined himself to the
doctrines which he might have extracted from the
bona fide works of Machiavelli, but has drawn extensively upon Gentillet in order to embody in a
single figure a typical Machiavellian. The best
evidence, of course, that Machiavelli was supposed
to be incarnated in the figure of Barabas is to be
obtained from the prologue itself, where such a
statement is directly made :

> *Machiavel.* Albeit the world thinks Machiavel is dead,
> Yet was his soul but flown beyond the Alps,
> And now the Guise is dead, is come from France,
> To view his land, and frolic with his friends.
> To some perhaps my name is odious,   5
> But such as love me guard me from their tongues ;
> And let them know that I am Machiavel,
> And weigh not men, and therefore not men's words.
> Admired I am of those that hate me most.
> Though some speak openly against my books,   10
> Yet they will read me, and thereby attain
> To Peter's chair : and when they cast me off
> Are poisoned by my climbing followers.
> I count religion but a childish toy,
> And hold there is no sin but ignorance.   15
> Birds of the air will tell of murders past !
> I am ashamed to hear such fooleries.

[1] The attempt to kill the Turks at a banquet may suggest
Thyestes, but has none of the gruesomeness of a human feast.
As a matter of fact the idea is that described in *The Prince* as
used by Oliverotto da Fermo.

Many will talk of title to a crown :
What right had Cæsar to the empery ?
Might first made kings, and laws were then most sure   20
When like the Draco's they were writ in blood.
Hence comes it that a strong-built citadel
Commends much more than letters can import ;
Which maxim had but Phalaris observed,
He had never bellowed, in a brazen bull,   25
Of great ones' envy. O' th' poor petty wights
Let me be envied and not pitied !
But whither am I bound ?   I come not, I,
To read a lecture here in Britain,
But to present the tragedy of a Jew   30
Who smiles to see how full his bags are crammed,
Which money was not got without my means.
I crave but this—grace him as he deserves,
And let him not be entertained the worse
Because he favours me.   35

Notice that the ghost, such a stock character in
the plays dominated by Senecan influence, is not to
be found in this prologue.   There is the spirit of a
dead man, but the spirit gives us no past history
that is necessary to an understanding of the play.
" Machiavel " simply states that he lives again in
the person of the Jew who is to play the leading
rôle in the ensuing tragedy, and gives us an advance
report of the character of Barabas as it later develops.
The prologue is an acknowledgment of the influence
of Machiavelli, and a guide to the nature of the
action.   It presumes Machiavellism to be pretty
well known and closely associated with the Guise,
to whose Machiavellian policy Gentillet, as we have
already seen, attributed the Massacre of St. Bartholomew.

Line 8 (above) is suggestive of Gentillet's maxim
I, of Part I :—" A Prince's good Counsell ought to
proceed from his owne wisedome, otherwise, he can-

not be well counselled." To a certain extent it also
draws upon the whole of Part III, especially 10, 18,
19, 22, 23. Lines 14 and 15 condense the thought
expressed in *The Prince*, 18, "but savour more of
Gentillet, II, 1."[1] The value of citadels (ll. 22–3
above) is discussed in *The Prince*, 20, and in Gentillet under III, 33. "In line 13 is the poison idea
fastened upon Machiavelli by Harvey, of whom
line 19 is also a reminiscence."[2]

That Machiavelli was generally supposed to have
advised the use of poison we have already learned.
Gentillet's maxim (III, 7) directing princes to
imitate Cæsar Borgia, Machiavelli's favourite, would
probably have suggested that Machiavelli approved
its use, at any rate.

Lines 18–21, especially the statement "Might
first made kings," embody what was then very
distinctly the popular notion of Machiavelli's
theory. In the opening chapter of *The Prince*, the
author says that "Principalities are either heredi-
tary . . . or but newly acquired"; and Chapter
III is largely taken up with a discussion of those
territories, ancient and modern, which were subjected by might to a foreign prince.

The speaker of the prologue calls attention to the
fact that Barabas' wealth was got by Machiavelli's
means (l. 32), a reminiscence of the Gentillet–
Patericke accusations. As Barabas pronounced

---

[1] Cf. Meyer, p. 40. The distinction between what is really
Machiavelli's and what Gentillet's will not be so closely drawn
as by Dr. Meyer, as our object is simply to point out ideas and
characteristics which the Elizabethans regarded as Machiavellian, whether justly so or not.

[2] See Meyer, p. 21, for Harvey.

himself a " Machiavel," and was popularly considered to be such indeed, avarice, usury, and great
wealth became closely associated with Machiavellism.

Barabas' advice to Ithamore,

> First be thou void of these affections,
> Compassion, love, vain hope, and heartless fear,
>
> (II, 157, Dyce ed.)

contains a true description of his own character,
but the lines immediately following, wherein he
sums up his past life, are probably to be taken as
the Jew's endeavour to impress Ithamore, rather
than as a true account. On the other hand, owing
to the fact that Barabas in the end tends to become
such a monster as he describes, the description may
be considered as embodying the popular conception
of a Machiavellian.

The number of murders in which Barabas has
a hand is astounding. He incites Lodowick and
Mathias to a fatal duel; strangles Friar Bernadine;
poisons his own daughter, all the nuns, Bellamira,
Ithamore, and Pilia Borsa ; besides plotting the
death of the entire Turkish force.

Other Machiavellian characteristics are equally
marked. He is patient under injury :

> No, Abigail ; things past recovery
> Are hardly cured with exclamations :
> Be silent, daughter ; sufferance breeds ease,
> And time may yield us an occasion,
> Which on the sudden cannot serve the turn. (I, 151.)

But he never forgets a wrong :

> I am not of the tribe of Levi, I,
> That can so soon forget an injury.   (II, 155.)

It is one of the maxims (III, 6) of Gentillet that princes and lords never forget an injury.

He does not believe the Christians are sincere :

> For I can see no fruits in all their faith,
> But malice, falsehood, and excessive pride,
> Which methinks fits not their profession. (I, 147.)

> Ay, policy, that's their profession,
> And not simplicity, as they suggest. (I, 150.)

He therefore considers himself perfectly justified in deceiving them :

> It's no sin to deceive a Christian ;
> For they themselves hold it a principle,
> Faith is not to be held with heretics :
> But all are heretics that are not Jews. (II, 159.)

Dissembling is second nature to him, and religion is professedly but a cloak to crime :

> She has confess'd, and we are both undone,
> My bosom inmate ! But I must dissemble.
>   (*Aside to Ithamore.*)
> O holy friars, the burdens of my sins
> Lie heavy on my soul ! Then pray you, tell me,
> Is't not too late now to turn Christian ? (IV, 166.)

> Ay, daughter ; for religion
> Hides many mischiefs from suspicion.
>   .   .   .   .
> As good dissemble what thou never mean'st
> As first mean truth and then dissemble it :
> A counterfeit profession is better
> Than unseen hypocrisy. (I, 151.)

Such religious hypocrisy is easily traceable to Gentillet, II, 1, 2 ; and *The Prince*, 18.

He admires treachery as well as hypocrisy :

>   Why, is not this
> A kingly kind of trade, to purchase towns
> By treachery, and sell 'em by deceit ? (V, 177.)

Compare this remark with Gentillet, III, 18, 21, 22, 23, 24.

He is an absolute egotist :

> Ego mihimet sum semper proximus.   (I, 148.)
> For so I live, perish may all the world.   (V, 177.)

" This is the very gist of Machiavelli's teachings,"
says Meyer.

He is subtle, of course, and looks a long way ahead :

> No, Barabas is born to better chance,
> And fram'd of finer mould than common men,
> That measure nought but by the present time.
> A reaching thought will search his deepest wits,
> And cast with cunning for the time to come ;
> For evils are apt to happen every day.   (I, 151.)

Although no political aspirant in the sense of
seeking the badge of office, he has a keen eye for
every advantage that may be gained by political
shrewdness :

> Thus hast thou gotten, by thy policy,
> No simple place, no small authority :
> I now am governor of Malta ; true,—
> But Malta hates me, and, in hating me,
> My life's in danger ; . . .   (V, 175.)

This speech will be recognized at once as Machiavellian. For Machiavelli's political treatise, written
purely for the guidance of a prince, points out not
only how he may establish a principality, but how
he may preserve himself in it. Barabas is simply
drawing the natural conclusion from the various
Machiavellian principles which he has enunciated :
since he cannot be a prince in safety he will be no
prince at all. Machiavelli asserts that a prince
must be of the nature of the lion and the fox.[1] As
Barabas is all fox he recognizes that he is not fit for
the position.

[1] *The Prince*, XVIII.

Two other incidents complete the cumulative evidence pointing to the influence of Machiavelli. Ithamore declares Barabas' acts to be under the control of the devil :

> Why, the devil invented a challenge, my master writ
> it, and I carried it. (III, 162.)

The opinion that Machiavelli was under the control of the devil had been seriously advanced as early as 1535 by Cardinal Pole,[1] and in the course of time became popular.

And, finally, Barabas dies cursing, as do the majority of later Machiavellian villains :

> Damn'd Christian dogs, and Turkish infidels !
> But now begins the extremity of heat
> To pinch me with intolerable pangs :
> Die, life ! fly, soul ! tongue, curse thy fill, and die !
> (V, 178.)

That Barabas was a Machiavellian according to the current notion is proved beyond a doubt. We find this to have been the general impression as late as the time of Heywood, who, editing *The Jew of Malta* in 1633, says in the prologue :

> . . . you shall find him still,
> In all his projects, a sound Machiavill ;
> And that's his character. (Dyce, 142.)

To sum up the characteristics of Barabas, we find him egotistical, cruel, faithless, remorseless, murderous, and a poisoner. These characteristics, many of which we found in Lorenzo, are important because they practically set the type for later villains. The plot, too, not in the particular incidents, but in general outline, is much the same as

---

[1] Epis. Reg. Pole : 1744, p. 136 ; quoted by Meyer, p. 5, note 3.

later ones representing the career of Machiavellians. The hero commences his tragic career out of hatred and revenge, pursues his plot by guile, but oversteps all bounds of justice and reason in the cruelty of his deeds, and is finally taken in his own toils and destroyed.

That the fall of such a man should fail to stir in us either pity or fear is to be expected ; but that a man in whom are to be found the above characteristics, calculated to produce only hatred, should at any stage of his career touch our sympathy, nay, more, rouse a wondering admiration, as Barabas does, is a matter for serious consideration. The explanation lies in the fact that Barabas is not *simply* evil ; along with the evil he has elements of greatness in his character, such as courage, intellect, and marked ability. Nietzsche, in *The Will to Power*, throws out a suggestion which deals with this very problem, and which cannot be ignored even by those who reject his philosophy as a whole. Under the heading " Optics of Valuation "[1] he states that our estimate of certain measures is affected by the following influences :

" The influence of the greatness or smallness of the aims.

" The influence of the intellectuality of the means.

" The influence of the behaviour in action.

" The influence of success or failure.

" The influence of opposing forces and their value.

" The influence of that which is permitted and that which is forbidden."

[1] *The Will to Power*, Vol. II, p. 223-4. Translated and edited by Dr. O. Levy. Published Macmillan.

Now this estimate of the influences that affect our measure of values is sound. It is perfectly true that in judging of men and actions we are influenced by the greatness of the aims, the intellectuality of the means, and the opposition to be overcome. And in *The Jew of Malta* Marlowe brings each of these influences to bear in such a way that he arouses for his hero both admiration and sympathy.

Soliloquies in particular are adopted as a means to produce this effect. In plays where the villain is the hero, soliloquies are necessary, because without them we should be deceived in the character of the villain. Under certain circumstances dialogues with accomplices might serve the same end as soliloquies ; but as accomplices are frequently unnecessary, and when used are commonly afterwards destroyed, soliloquy becomes our only means of discovering the purpose of the villain. For the means whereby he gains his ends is deception, and we should be deceived along with his dupes but for soliloquy. Consequently, the suspense necessary to dramatic emotion would be wanting, and the deeds of the villain would come upon us as shocking surprises. Soliloquy is still more necessary if we are to have any sympathy with the villain. In his soliloquies he pictures the height of his ambition or the depth of his injuries, and so arouses a certain admiration or sympathy with which we can accompany him part way, at least, on his career of crime.

By just such means does Barabas win our respect. His ambition is glorious ; even his egotism and pride have their admirable side ; while his grief and indignation at the outrage perpetrated upon him

predispose us to sympathize with his desire for
revenge. When Barabas is introduced to us in the
counting-house his wealth is represented as so
enormous and his ambition so vast that, as Bullen
says, "our senses are dazzled, sober reason is
staggered."

> Give me the merchants of the Indian mines,
> That trade in metal of the purest mould ;   20
> The wealthy Moor, that in the eastern rocks
> Without control can pick his riches up,
> And in his house heap pearls like pebble-stones,
> Receive them free and sell them by the weight ;
> Bags of fiery opals, sapphires, amethysts,   25
> Jacinths, hard topaz, grass-green emeralds,
> Beauteous rubies, sparkling diamonds,
> And seld-seen costly stones of so great price,
> As one of them, indifferently rated,
> And of a carat of this quantity,   30
> May serve in peril of calamity
> To ransom great kings from captivity.

There is no grovelling, miserly greed in such a
passion as this. It is the ambition of a Faustus for
infinite power expressed in terms of gold. The man
who is capable of such a stupendous conception of
wealth has within him an imagination that commands our admiration, if it does not touch us with
awe. Nor is Barabas a mere dreamer ; he actually
possesses such wealth :

> This is the ware wherein consists my wealth.   33

Moreover, he uses it in such a manner as to make
him more powerful than kings :

> What more may Heaven do for earthly man
> Than thus to pour out plenty in their laps,
> Ripping the bowels of the earth for them,
> Making the seas their servants and the winds
> To drive their substance with successful blasts.

.   .   .   .   .

I must confess we come not to be kings ;
That's not our fault : alas, our number's few,
And crowns come either by succession,
Or urged by force ; and nothing violent,
Oft have I heard tell, can be permanent.
Give us a peaceful rule, make Christians kings,
That thirst so much for principality.

Barabas is not only the richest of the Jews, but the proudest. He feels himself coequal in dignity with princes, and born to rule, though peacefully withal. It is something to command the mines, to rule the seas, and to govern the commerce of the world. Thus by appealing to our love of power does Marlowe awaken our admiration for the Jew, while he refines and softens his character by the bursts of lyric poetry which he causes to spring from his lips.

To the powerful, and to the imaginative elements which go to make up the character of Barabas must be added tenderness, family affection, which is called forth in his relations with his daughter. These are the admirable elements which exist side by side with the evil in his nature. But how do they enable us to forgive his crimes ?

Barabas fascinates us in the first instance, as we have already seen, not only by the actual but by the latent power that seems to exist within him. But this man of great capacities is an outcast from society, a member of an oppressed race, who is subjected to indignity and gross injustice by those vested with authority, to whom he has given not the slightest offence.

Who hateth me but for my happiness ?

he justly exclaims. His oppressors arouse not the slightest sympathy in us, for they are not psychologized by the dramatist. Consequently, when they treat the Jew shabbily we are full of sympathy for him. The burst of wrath with which he turns on his meek spirited brethren for yielding so quickly to extortion reveals his own high spirit and warms us to him :

> O earth-mettled villains, and no Hebrews born !
> And will you basely thus submit yourself
> To leave your goods to their arbitrament ?

Resistance by force being impossible, and justice for a Jew unheard of, we are at one with him in his desire for revenge when his goods are taken from him. Guile being the only weapon left him ceases to carry with it the usual imputation of servility and baseness. Barabas' guileful acts, therefore, instead of signifying depravity and alienating sympathy, point to a fertile wit and a spirit not easily tamed.

> *Bar.* You partial heavens, have I deserved
>   this plague ?
> What, will you oppose me, luckless stars,
> To make me desperate in my poverty ?
> And knowing me impatient in distress,
> Think me so mad as I will hang myself,
> That I may vanish o'er the earth in air,
> And leave no memory that e'er I was ?
> No, I will live ; nor loathe I this my life :
> And since you leave me in the ocean thus
> To sink or swim, and put me to my shifts,
> I'll rouse my senses and awake myself.

Here are the egotism and pride of Barabas transformed to a courage which touches our sympathies. Even in the revenge which follows, in the taking of life, he has our sympathetic understanding though not our moral sanction. For he, a man of self-respect and intellect, has been wounded in his sorest point, and humiliated, not by one man, in which case he might have limited his revenge or asked for justice, but by a race which he despises ; wherefore his hatred extends to the whole race.

Barabas only loses his tragic hold upon us after the psychologic basis for his actions disappears. But he then degenerates from a man of ability and courage, spurred on to revenge by wounded pride and a sense of outrage, into the mere caricature of a man, a bloodthirsty monster, a being delighting in devilish intrigue for its own sake, exhibiting himself in positions that are grotesque, accomplishing the most improbable feats, and contriving the most fantastic plots.

In the first two acts the character of Barabas is treated seriously ; he is represented as a man capable of deep feeling, and his love for his daughter is portrayed as one of the deepest passions of his life. In Act III he learns from a letter that Abigail has entered a convent, and Ithamore assures him that the report is true. Now note the rapid change in feeling :

> *Bar.*   O unhappy day !
> False, credulous, inconstant Abigail !
> But let 'em go : And, Ithamore, from hence
> Ne'er shall she grieve me more with her disgrace ;
> Ne'er shall she live to inherit aught of mine,
> Be blest of me, nor come within my gates,
> But perish underneath my bitter curse,
> Like Cain by Adam for his brother's death.
>   *Ith.*   O master !
>   *Bar.*   Ithamore, entreat not for her, I am moved,
> And she is hateful to my soul and me ;
> And 'less thou yield to this that I entreat,
> I cannot think but that thou hat'st my life.
>   (III, iv.)

Whereupon he immediately conceives the plot of poisoning his daughter and all the nuns by a pot of porridge. Here is an abrupt change of character indeed ! We do not insist that grief as well as rage should be represented in the language of Barabas, but we do insist that he could be so passionately moved by his daughter's flight to the side of his oppressors only if he loved her passionately, and that his attempt to poison her under such circumstances is manifestly contrary to human nature. And the manner in which he goes about these later crimes ! The dignified Barabas of Acts I and II transformed to the Barabas of the rice-mixing scene of Act III is an absurdity ; and the device by which the poison reaches its destination strains the limits of probability. Barabas has been changed from a man into a monster, and serious tragedy turned into melodrama ; grotesque and melodramatic elements dominate the rest of the play. The incident of the friars belongs to farce, not to tragedy ; Barabas as the butt of the cut-purse Pilia-Borsa and the drunken Ithamore is ludicrous, not dignified or pathetic ; the incident of his taking a sleeping potion and being thrown over the walls out of harm's way and without injury is absurd ; it is merely inserted to put him in a position for further plotting. If the dramatist had brought about the Jew's conspiracy with the Turks against Malta in a logical and reasonable manner, it would have been eminently tragic and quite in keeping with the hatred and intellectual astuteness of Barabas, but tossing him in a drugged condition over the wall to bring about this end is machinery of the grossest kind. Then the grotesque scheme of letting the Turks down through a trap-door into a boiling cauldron—how untragic ! And how improbable that a man so shrewd as Barabas should release his worst enemy and put himself in his power ! Such actions are too unnatural to find a place in anything but the most sensational and agonizing melodrama.

After the second act Barabas does nothing in keeping with his character, and the events are brought about without logical sequence. Consequently, in spite of our sympathy for the Jew in the beginning, when the play closes we experience no tragic emotion.

VI

THE AMBITIOUS VILLAIN-HERO

THE villain-hero plays that follow *The Jew of Malta* fall into one of two classes, according as the motive which dominates the hero is ambition or revenge. Barabas was by nature ambitious, but, as we have seen, most of his actions were the result of a desire for revenge. His enemies blocked his ambition; so he turned to retaliation. There were a number of plays produced shortly after *The Jew of Malta*, however, in which the villain-heroes are swayed altogether by ambition. These heroes share all the guileful Machiavellian characteristics of Barabas, but they turn them to ambitious ends, even to conquering foreign lands. Now, the love of conquest that marks these protagonists was probably derived from Tamburlaine. Tamburlaine is a Machiavellian, indeed,[1] but he is a conquering hero, not a villain, and hence does not fall within the scope of this discussion.[2] Moreover, he is all lion and no fox; he does not illustrate the subtlety and treachery associated with Machiavellism as does Barabas. The dramatists who follow in the wake of Marlowe in creating

[1] Cf. Meyer, p. 34, quoting Brandl.
[2] In the Preface I have explained that the moral standards that prevail in time of peace are not accepted in time of war, especially if the war is one of foreign conquest.

ambitious villains try to combine the qualities of both of Marlowe's heroes. They may wish to produce a conqueror play, but that is not enough ; the conquering hero must also be full of guile, he must commit such atrocities in private life as will render him a villain. On the other hand, there are a few plays in which the hero's one passion is a towering ambition consummated by Machiavellian wiles, but in which foreign conquest has no place. If these latter plays were not inspired by a first-hand knowledge of Machiavelli or Gentillet, they are indebted more to *The Jew of Malta* than to *Tamburlaine*. For, let me repeat, what the Elizabethans thought of as Machiavellism is much more pronounced in the character of Barabas than in that of Tamburlaine.

Orlando Furioso, one of the earliest villain-hero plays of the conqueror type, serves as an excellent foil to bring out the characteristics evidently considered most typical of Machiavellism. The play, which traces its source to Ariosto, has been considered as a parody on the " mad plays " popular at that time,[1] but Sacripant, the leading figure in the play, is no less a parody on the Machiavellian villain-hero. Although the date of composition is not fixed,[2] the play contains so many scenes which make excellent parodies of *Tamburlaine* and *The Jew of Malta* that it must have been written after them. No hero ever had higher aspirations than Sacripant ; no villain ever adopted more ignoble means to attain his ends. Both as hero and villain,

[1] Cf. T. H. Dickinson, Introduction, Mermaid ed.
[2] Acted 1592, according to Henslowe.

however, he is ridiculed.   The mock-heroic style of
his first soliloquy is a travesty of Tamburlaine :

> And when I set my bonnet on my head,
> Methinks I fit my forehead for a crown.
>
> .   .   .   .   .
>
> My dreams are princely, all of diadems.
>
> .   .   .   .
>
> These please the ear, and with a sweet applause,
> Make me in terms coequal with the gods.
>
> (p. 177, Mermaid ed.)

Here we have the Machiavellian principles of
egotism and the will to power pushed to a ludicrous
extreme.   Likewise his speech to his man (p. 178)
revealing his intentions and principles is clearly
dictated by Machiavellian policy :

> Foe unto both, friend only to myself,
> And to the crown, for that's the golden mark
> Which makes my thoughts dream on a diadem.

When his man asks for his method of obtaining
the crown, he replies (p. 178) :

> That's to be done by poison, prowess, or any means
> of treachery.

He dies with a tremendous burst of egotism :

> Heaven, earth, men, beasts, and every living thing,
> Consume and end with County Sacripant.   (p. 215.)

The maxims and principles placed in the mouth
of Sacripant show that the author of the play was
undoubtedly familiar with some of the works of
Machiavelli ;   while the fact that these principles
were used for the purpose of burlesque, shows just
as conclusively that the general public must have
been familiar with stage characters whose claim to
heroism was based upon their imitation of Machia-

vellian policy. Otherwise, what is apparently burlesque would be mere silliness. Burlesque, to have any effect, must apply to something well known. This very burlesque treatment, however, of Sacripant's ambition, which shows that the character-type was well known, renders serious study of the tragic effect of his ambition super-fluous.

One of the serious plays of this type, and possibly by the same author as *Orlando Furioso*, but of un-certain date, is *Selimus*. Selimus, the villain-hero, partakes of the nature of both Tamburlaine and Barabas. He plots and murders with the one, while he marches on to conquest with the other. He gains our attention as the central figure in the first place by Bajazet's introductory description of his character, and then by himself telling us what he believes and disbelieves, what he is capable of and what he intends to do. His actions are in perfect harmony with the character revealed in soliloquy. The darling of the soldiers, because of warlike prowess, he is proclaimed emperor by them during his father's lifetime. He at once poisons his father, Bajazet, as being a latent source of trouble; strangles Corcut, eldest son of Bajazet; strangles Mustapha and his wife for trying to save the children of the second son, Acomat; then murders Acomat's wife after taking her city; marches against the allied forces of Acomat and the Egyptian prince; defeats them; kills his brother, and so ends the play.

The play is a chronicle of contemporary foreign history, and shares the undramatic element of all chronicles, in being a mere succession of scenes.

The taste of the audience for bloody themes is naively suggested in the " Conclusion " by the author :

> Thus have we brought victorious Selimus
> Unto the crown of great Arabia ;
> Next, shall you see him with triumphant sword,
> Dividing kingdoms into equal shares,
> And give them to his warlike followers.
> If this part, Gentiles, do like you well,
> The second part shall greater murthers tell.

We have been spared the second part.

Cunliffe has pointed out the influence of Seneca upon this tragedy as a whole : " The play opens with reflections on the cares and uncertainties of empire quite in the style of the Roman dramatist and philosopher. The description of the golden age may be paralleled by *Hippolytus*, 533–57 ; and the sceptical reasoning that follows by *Troas*, 380–417. Then we have Sisyphus, Ixion, and ' the cave of damned ghoasts ' with which Seneca has made us familiar, and later on are confronted by ' all the damned monsters of black hell.' Seneca's dialogue is successfully imitated, and sometimes not only the style, but the matter also is borrowed. . . . Some of the situations may also have been suggested by Seneca, but this is more doubtful."[1]

Seneca undoubtedly exercised an influence over this drama, but in none of Cunliffe's quotations of dialogue, nor in any of the situations referred to, do we find the person of Selimus. Of the two bloody brothers, Acomat is the more cruel, taking delight in mutilation and suffering after the manner of Senecan villains, while Selimus is fashioned more

---

[1] *The Influence of Seneca*, p. 63 ff.

closely after a Machiavellian model. He is ambitious
and takes to heart Machiavelli's advice to maintain
a principality by fear rather than love :

> Now, Selimus, consider who thou art ;   235
> Long hast thou marchèd in disguis'd attire,
> But now unmask thyself, and play thy part,
> And manifest the heat of thy desire ;
> Nourish the coals of thine ambitious fire ;
> And think that then thy empire is most sure,   240
> When men for fear thy tyranny endure,
> Think that to thee there is no worse reproach,
> Than filial duty in so high a place.
> Thou oughtst to set barrels of blood abroach,
> And seek with sword whole kingdoms to displace. 245
>   (Temple ed.)

Notice how closely lines 240–1 and 244–5, above,
parallel in wording and sentiment the verses
of Machiavel in the Prologue of *The Jew of
Malta* :

> Might first made kings, and laws were then most sure
> When like the Draco's they were writ in blood.

Selimus is also an atheist and scoffs at religion :

> I count it sacrilege, for to be holy,
> Or reverence this thread-bare name of good ;   250
> Leave to old men and babes that kind of folly,
> Count it of equal value with the mud :
> Make thou a passage for thy gushing flood,
> By slaughter, treason, or what else thou can,
> And scorn religion ; it disgraces man.

He thinks that religion had its origin in policy :

> Then some sage man, above the vulgar wise,   330
> Knowing that laws could not in quiet dwell
> Unless they were observed, did first devise
> The names of Gods, religion, heaven, and hell,
> And 'gan of pains, and feign'd rewards to tell ;
> Pains for those men who did neglect the law,   335
> Rewards, for those who lived in quiet awe.

> Whereas indeed, they were mere fictions,
> And if they were not Selim thinks they were ;
> And these religious observations,
> Only bug-bears to keep the world in fear,   340
> And make men quietly a yoke to bear.
> So that religion, of itself a bauble,
> Was only found to make us peaceable.

This is just the kind of cynicism for which Gentillet censured Machiavelli. We find more of the policy idea in the following :

> So this is well : for I am none of those
> That make a conscience for to kill a man.   1730
> For nothing is more hurtful to a prince,
> Than to be scrupulous and religious.
> I like Lysander's counsel passing well ;
> ' If that I cannot speed with lion's force,
> To clothe my complots in a fox's skin.'   1735
> For th' only things that wrought our empery[1]
> Were open wrongs and hidden treachery.
> Oh ! th' are two wings wherewith I use to fly,
> And soar above the common sort.
> If any seek our wrongs to remedy,   1740
> With these I take his meditation short ;
> And one of these shall still maintain my cause,
> Or fox's skin or lion's rending paws.

Although the citation of Lysander shows that the author of this play had read Plutarch and there came upon the idea of the lion and the fox,[2] yet the same idea is to be found in Machiavelli, while the other passages we have quoted, with their laudation of fraud, murder, and hypocrisy, leave no doubt that Selimus should be classed with the type of Machiavellian villain already staged by

[1] Compare this phraseology with that of the Prologue of *The Jew of Malta* :
> What right had Cæsar to the empery ?
> Might first made kings . . .

[2] Plutarch, ed. Langh., 295.

Marlowe. It is not, however, by plots of retaliation that he wins our attention, but by high-handed deeds of ambition. He feels his own strength and wants to be king. He is at once remorseless, conscienceless, and powerful. He kills every one who stands in his way to the throne or who is likely to cause trouble after he gains it. He knows neither love, pity, nor hatred ; he fears neither man, God, nor devil ; but takes the nearest way to gratify his lust for empire. Any form of murder appeals to him, poisoning, stabbing, or strangling. But he does not gloat in torture like his brother Acomat, who reminds one of Aaron or Eleazar in such cruelties as cutting off the hands and tongue of Aga. He boasts of his crimes, his atheism, and his power like Barabas ; in the removal of impediments he is as ruthless as Richard III, but is less subtle, less intellectual, and has fewer odds to contend with. Wicked as this man is, however, his villainy does not affect our passions. The reason we do not hate him is because his father is weak, his brother Acomat worse than himself, and Corcut a nonentity. We do not fear him, because he is not humanized ; he remains a mere figure with traits of character pinned on the outside—like Almanzor, in *The Conquest of Granada*. The only difference between Selimus and Dryden's hero is that, though both are always successful, Almanzor is always good and Selimus never is.

The language used in the play by the various persons, and the acts performed, show the force at work upon the dramatists of that period—viz. the demand of the people for violent deeds and striking characters, such as were to be found in Senecan and Machiavellian sources. The author of *Selimus* gave them what they wanted, but produced a most inferior tragedy. In the modern acceptation of the word it is no tragedy at all, because the hero does not meet with misfortune. As the hero in this case is a villain of the deepest dye, it would be rather shocking to our moral sense to have the play close with him triumphant if it were not for the fact above stated that the drama is a chronicle in which none of the characters is psychologized. We sit through an exhibition of rather exciting situations, but are never deeply moved one way or the other. Without the element of strong characterization, the succession of events has no casual sequence and the result stirs no tragic emotion.

Ambition is likewise the ruling motive in Fulke Greville's *Alaham*. No positive date can be assigned for this play; what little evidence there is indicates that it was not written later than 1600, though it may have been written ten years earlier.[1] Alaham is a villain and the hero, but the tragedy presents serious difficulties on account of its obscurity and because it is so undramatic—the author admitting that it was not written to be acted. As far as the outline of the action is concerned, however, it fits in admirably with the type of play we have been studying. Alaham is the second son of a weak king whose eldest son and heir to the throne is feeble-minded. Alaham commences his tragic career from ambition. He usurps the throne, blinds his father

---

[1] *Works of Fulke Greville*, pp. 22 and 41, M. W. Croll, Penn. Thesis, 1903.

and brother, and later burns them, together with his sister, who tries to protect them ; but at the moment of triumph he meets his own death by a poisoned coronation robe, the gift of his wife whose paramour he had executed. This outline suggests a very blood-curdling play quite in line with *Selimus*, except for the martial conquests of the one and the fatal ending of the other. And yet the author was trying to avoid giving an impression of the terror of lawlessness and might. He says : [1]

" Now to return to the Tragedies remaining, my purpose in them was not (with the Ancient) to exemplifie the disastrous miseries of man's life where Order, Lawes, Doctrine, and Authority are unable to protect Innocencey from the exorbitant wickednesse of power, and so out of that melancholike Vision, stir [up] horrour, or murmur against Divine Providence : nor yet (with the Moderne) to point out God's revenging aspect upon every particular sin, to the despaire, or confusion of mortality ; but rather to trace out the high waies of ambitious Governours, and to shew in the practice, that the more audacity, advantage, and good successe such Soveraignties have, the more they hasten to their owne desolation and ruine."

It is curious that Greville, endeavouring to avoid " the disastrous miseries of man's life where Order, Lawes, Doctrine, and Authority are unable to protect Innocencey," should have portrayed a typical Machiavellian villain, a type which other dramatists chose chiefly because of the fascinating situations made possible by the triumph of guileful

---

[1] *Life of Sidney,* ed. Grosart, p. 320 ff.

wickedness over innocent simplicity. For Alaham actually bears the stamp of the other villains we have studied, being egotistical, guileful, cruel, faithless, remorseless, and murderous.

Greville's design, as above set forth, is in itself not undramatic, and, as a matter of fact, Alaham's death follows as effect upon cause, but instead of resulting from the " audacity, advantage, and good successe " of such a sovereign, as Greville intended, it follows simply from the execution of a wicked minister, his wife's paramour, who in revenge murders her husband, thus imitating, in construction at least, the most sensational elements in the Senecan-Machiavellian tragedies. The attempt to revive classical tragedy results in a hero who is a villain much like Selimus. The difference between the heroes modelled after Marlowe and those of the classical reversionists is, after all, not great. The distinction lies in the rest of the play—in the moral sentiments, the dialogue, and the suppression of the romantic element. If theorizing had not been the author's avowed object, the tragedy would have afforded a good test of the emotional effect of a tragedy in which the villain was hero. For, owing to the fact that Alaham's father was weak, and his brother unfit to rule, while at the same time the kingdom was being actually mismanaged by corrupt ministers, we could have sympathized with the ambitious son's desire to take the reins of government into his own hands. As it is, however, the plot is not at all indicative of the nature of the tragedy, for the author disregards the primary law of the drama, namely, action. There are only two

dramatic scenes in the whole play, the one where
the daughter leads the blind king and tries to protect him,[1] the other where Hala in the presence of
Alaham slays Cain's child thinking it her own and
Alaham's.[2]   For the rest, the tragedy resembles
more approximately a philosophical dissertation on
statecraft, cast in dramatic form, than drama itself.
Long dialogues and soliloquies are given over to
elaborate argumentation while the action remains
at a standstill.   Even in the last act where Alaham
puts on the poisoned robe which is the cause of his
death, the author takes no advantage of the situation.   After remarking

> The poison works ; I feel my spirits faint,

the hero pays no further attention to the poison,
but devotes his few remaining moments to marvel-
ling at the horrible revelation that a woman could
kill her own child.

A puppet could be made to play the part of
Alaham just as effectively as a human actor ; he
leaves absolutely no impression of personality upon
us ; he is devoid of emotion himself, and so arouses
none in us.   It would be difficult to find another
play containing an account of similar ambition,
consummated by such crimes, that one could read
with so much indifference, so little emotion.   Even
the impression of horror is but fleeting.   The failure
of the play as a tragedy is in no sense due to the fact
that a villain is the hero, but to the fact that there
is no action and no characterization.

In the *Massacre at Paris* (acted 1592–3) another

---

[1] Suggestive of *Œdipus*.   [2] Suggestive of *Medea*.

villain is presented as hero in the person of the
Duke of Guise.   As early as 1576 Gentillet had
associated this massacre with the name of the
Guise, as an example of the terrible effects of
Machiavellian policy.   In the play under consideration, however, although Machiavellian elements are
distinctly present, lack of characterization and clear
motivation confuses the issues involved.   In an
early part of the play a soaring ambition, with a
touch of Tamburlaine in it, seems to be the Guise's
ruling motive, if we may judge from his soliloquies :

> *Guise.*   Now, Guise, begin those deep engendered
>   thoughts
> To burst abroad those never-dying flames
> Which cannot be extinguished but by blood.
> Oft have I levelled, and at last have learn'd
> That peril is the chiefest way to happiness,
> And resolution honor's fairest aim.
> What glory is there in a common good,
> That hangs for every peasant to achieve ?
> That like I best that flies beyond my reach.
> Let me to scale the high pyramids,
> And thereon set the diadem of France ;
> I'll either rend it with my nails to naught,
> Or mount the top with my aspiring wings,
> Although my downfall be the deepest hell.
> For this I wake, when others think I sleep ;
> For this I wait, that scorn attendance else ;
> For this, my quenchless thirst, whereon I build,
> Hath often pleaded kindred to the king ;
> For this, this head, this heart, this hand, this sword,
> Contrives, imagines, and fully executes,
> Matters of import aimed at by many
> Yet understood by none ;
> For this, hath heaven engendered me of earth ;
> For this, this earth sustains my body's weight,
> And with this weight I'll counterpoise a crown,

Or with seditions weary all the world ;
For this, from Spain the stately Catholics
Send Indian gold to coin me French ecues ;
For this, have I a largess from the Pope,
A pension, and a dispensation too ;
And by that privilege to work upon,
My policy hath fram'd religion.
Religion ! *O Diabole !*
Fie, I am asham'd, however that I seem,
To think a word of such a simple sound,
Of so great matter should be made the ground !
The gentle king, whose pleasure uncontroll'd
Weakeneth his body, and will waste his realm,
If I repair not what he ruinates,—
Him, as a child, I daily win with words,
So that for proof he barely bears the name ;
I execute, and he sustains the blame.
The mother-queen works wonders for my sake,
And in my love entombs the hope of France,
Rifling the bowels of her treasury,
To supply my wants and necessity.
Paris hath full five hundred colleges,
As monasteries, priories, abbeys, and halls,
Wherein are thirty thousand able men
Besides a thousand sturdy student Catholics :
And more,—of my knowledge, in one cloister keep
Five hundred fat Franciscan friars and priests :
All this and more, if more may be comprised,
To bring the will of our desires to end.
Then, Guise,
Since thou hast all the cards within thy hands,
To shuffle or cut, take this as surest thing,
That, right or wrong, thou deal thyself a king.—
Ay, but Navarre,—'tis but a nook of France,
Sufficient yet for such a petty king,
That, with a rabblement of his heretics,
Blinds Europe's eyes, and troubleth our estate.
Him will we (*pointing to his sword*)—but first let's follow
    those in France

That hinder our possession to the crown.
As Cæsar to his soldiers, so say I,—
Those that hate me will I learn to loathe.
Give me a look, that, when I bend the brows,
Pale death may walk in furrows of my face ;
A hand, that with a grasp may gripe the world ;
An ear to hear what my detractors say ;
A royal seat, a sceptre, and a crown ;
That those who do behold, they may become
As men that stand and gaze against the sun.
The plot is laid, and things shall come to pass
Where resolution strives for victory.

> (End of **Sc.** 2, Bullen's ed.)

This speech, it will be noted, reveals another Machiavellian trait besides ambition—religious hypocrisy ; (the Guise feigns religious zeal in order to advance and conceal his personal ambition) He also, in the course of the play, poisons the Queen of Navarre, and murders the Admiral, besides instigating and taking part in the massacre itself. If we were to judge from the above-quoted soliloquy alone, we should conclude that these actions were but the Machiavellian means of realizing a Machiavellian ambition for political power. But the Guise is very serious in his crimes, as we see when he turns from his greater ambition, after Henry comes to the throne, to resent a private insult by murder. Now, the real Machiavellian whose object is to be a prince, commits his crimes in a rather jocund spirit as if men were so many flies. The thing that makes it difficult to class the Guise as a Machiavellian is that in spite of his ambition and his sneer at religion he appears from his actions to be a religious fanatic, the art of the dramatist yielding at this point to popular prejudice. As we follow him through the play sheer hatred of Protestantism seems to be the inflaming force rather than ambition, and this detracts from the craftiness and intriguing by which Machiavellians centre our attention on themselves. When he dies, his curses fall as heavily on the Huguenots as on individuals.

> Pope excommunicate, Philip, depose
> The wicked branch of curs'd Valois his line !
> Vive la messe ! perish Huguenots !
> Thus Cæsar did go forth and thus he died. (Sc. 21.)

The Guise is ambitious, guileful, cruel, faithless, murderous, remorseless, and a poisoner; but the element of religious fanaticism in his character is too realistically portrayed to permit of his being classed as an egotist and an atheist. Consequently he lacks two requisites of a Machiavellian villain-hero.

Although not a complete Machiavellian, the Guise is nevertheless a villain and the protagonist. But he arouses no tragic emotion. This is due to deficient characterization, the mixture of motives, and the lack of unity. The play is a chronicle on contemporary foreign history, and the author feels that he can leave nothing out. Kings are made and unmade and events crowded together with total disregard of the unity of action or logical sequence ; characters are portrayed according to popular prejudice, the hated Catholics placed in an ugly light, and all horrors carefully preserved, with no respect for consistency. The result is neither history nor tragedy, but confusion.

The True Tragedy of Richard III (1589-91) [1] introduces a villain-hero who appears again more highly developed in Shakespeare's tragedy. Richard of *The True Tragedy* shows the influence of both *Tamburlaine* [2] and Machiavelli. In his love of power and of himself, his disinclination to trust anyone but himself, his reliance on fear rather than love as a maxim of government, and in his murders he is a Machiavellian. But he depends chiefly on force, as does Tamburlaine, and in the play has little occasion for craft, although he is supposed to be treacherous. His character is somewhat studied, much more so than Alaham's, but in spite of a good deal of evidence that the author tried to rivet attention upon the force of character in a single figure rather than upon the history of a reign, the scenes are more epic, i.e. chronological, than dramatic. The attempt at characterization, taken all in all, is a failure.

The first soliloquy [3] represents the process of transition in Richard's mind from desire for the crown to strong determination to get it, in a manner that puts character into the mental struggle. In the last soliloquy Richard is dogged by remorse, which begins as soon as he obtains the crown. But what takes place in the intervening acts is jerky and disconnected. Buckingham quarrels with Rivers all unexpectedly ; the Queen flies to sanctuary before the occasion for her so doing—the arrest of her kinsmen—has occurred ; the Cardinal's appearance

[1] *Richard the Third up to Shakespeare*, by G. B. Churchill. Palæstra X.

[2] Churchill, *ibid.*

[3] *The True Tragedy of Richard III*, ed. Baron Fields, p. 14.

demanding young York, and the mother's sudden
yielding, constitute a surprise ; Hastings is carried
away to prison without our having had an opportunity to study in Richard the development of
purpose which brings this action about ; Buckingham is very suddenly arrested as a traitor without
our knowing that he had ever broken with Richard.
We finally learn the reasons for all these unexpected
happenings from the Page, but the explanations
usually come after the event, as, for example, in
the scene where the Page reports the manner in
which Richard took the field and met his death,
after we have seen him die.   As a result, we have
no chance to study Richard's mind.   On one occasion, indeed, he confides to the Page in advance
that he wants to murder the children, but his language when " 'tis out," is that of a swashbuckler,
as it is in many other dialogues.   Although the first
and the last soliloquies make a very fair beginning
and ending in character study, a complete character
is not represented ; for we are not let into the
subtleties of Richard's mind in the meantime, nor
prepared for the disintegration of character that is
presupposed in the last soliloquy.

The inferiority of the play as a whole aids in
depriving the character of Richard of verisimilitude.
Not only does the author present instead of a tragedy
a mere series of scenes shifted with marvellous
rapidity, but he manifests no dramatic sense in his
selection of scenes.   The most trivial are given an
equal place with the most important, and those
actions which are reported by the Page are nearly
all of more importance dramatically than those

that are actually staged. About the only value of such a play for our purposes is to show that the heroic villain was being kept before the public, and that the author was conscious that such a figure ought to be psychologized, although he was unable to rise to the occasion himself.

VII

AMBITIOUS HERO CONTINUED
THE PERFECTED TYPE—RICHARD III

In *Richard III* (1592–4) we come for the first time
to a villain-hero play which grips us from beginning
to end, which is really a tragedy. The motive which
governs Shakespeare's hero is ambition. He combines the lust of power found in Tamburlaine with
a guile and intellectual astuteness far surpassing
that of Barabas. But with it all the character of
Richard is real ; he is the first real villain we have
had. His murders are no less atrocious than those of
Selimus, his aspirations no more extraordinary ; but
the secret of Richard's reality—for we actually
speak and think of him as a person—lies, it seems
to me, in the naturalness of his speeches. He does
not spurn the earth every time he opens his lips,
but, on the contrary, speaks simply, just as we
should expect a man of his character to speak. Hence
his success or failure seems profoundly significant.

Richard is the perfect Machiavellian. Tamburlaine and Barabas are both one-sided, but Richard
combines all the traits necessary to a successful
prince, according to Machiavelli. Indeed, he is
able to " set the murd'rous Machiavel to school,"[1]
which is not unnatural, as it was from such historical

[1] 3 *Henry VI*, III, 2 (193).

characters as Richard III that Machiavelli drew his models. The Richard of the play is lacking in only one thing to conform absolutely to Machiavelli's ideal, and that is statesmanship. Machiavelli does not advise a prince to murder indiscriminately, with no care for the state, but advises the use of murder if it is necessary to produce a well-ordered state. The Richard of history actually reigned for a number of years as an able statesman, which would have been Machiavelli's justification for citing him ; but the Richard of the play is overthrown as soon as intrenched, and it is his criminal nature, not his ability as a ruler, which is portrayed.

Richard is an absolute hypocrite, but never deceives himself. The proudest man that ever breathed, he yet says in the reconciliation scene brought about by the dying Edward :

> 'Tis death for me to be at enmity ;
> I hate it, and desire all good men's love.
>
> I thank my God for my humility.   (II, i, 72.)

He uses religion simply to advance his cause, as witness his stand between the two bishops, Prayer Book in hand, when the citizens, led by Buckingham, come to urge him to accept the crown (III, vii).

Or note what he says in soliloquy :

> I do the wrong and first begin the brawl.
> The secret mischiefs that I set abroach
> I lay unto the grievous charge of others.
>
> But then I sigh ; and, with a piece of Scripture,
> Tell them that God bids us do good for evil :
> And thus I clothe my naked villainy
> With old odd ends stolen out of holy writ :
> And seem a saint, when most I play the devil.
>   (I, iii.)

He scoffs at conscience :

Conscience is but a word that cowards use.

He destroys his accomplices as well as all of those who in any way interfere with his advancement. As Richmond puts it, he is

One raised in blood, and one in blood established ;
One that made means to come by what he hath,
And slaughtered those that were the means to help him.
(V, iii.)

He is also a consummate egotist.

Over and above all these traits, which Barabas possessed, Richard unites in himself the natures of the lion and the fox, and rules his conduct by those maxims written solely for the use of princes, for which Barabas, being no prince, had no use.[1]

Although Barabas approaches Richard in guile, and although Selimus is his equal in courage, neither of them can compare with him in intellectuality or versatility. Strength of intellect is the very essence of Richard's character, and there can be no doubt that his versatility, which has made his part so popular among actors, is more pronounced than that of any other hero of the tragic drama.

Summing up his characteristics, good and bad, we find that he is fearless, egotistical, haughty, audacious, subtle, witty, intellectual, bold, treacherous, far-sighted, remorseless, atheistical, cynical, and above all gifted with almost superhuman energy of will. He does not use poison, but with this exception we find that he possesses every Machiavellian trait.

[1] To understand how thoroughly Machiavellian Richard's ruling principles really are, compare them with Gentillet's maxims, I, 1, 3 ; II, 1 ; III, 4, 8, 9, 10, 11, 12, 18, 19, 21, 23.

The prevalence of blood and violence that we have come to regard as Senecan is also characteristic of the drama of *Richard III*. But this may be mere coincidence, for the incidents are taken from English history. At any rate, it may be said that national history, popular taste, and Senecan precedent all justified the bloodshed and violent natures represented in this tragedy. Cunliffe (p. 72 ff.) sees Senecan influence manifesting itself in a more specific manner. He says, for instance, that both Seneca and Shakespeare urge frequently the cares and risks of high places and the benefits of obscurity, both put forward the idea of the presentiment of evil, to which "may be added another commonplace of morality which occurs more than once in each poet:"

> Uncertain way of gain ! But I am in
> So far in blood that sin will pluck on sin.
> *(Richard III*, IV, 2.)
>
> Per scelera semper sceleribus tutum est iter.
> *(Agamemnon*, 116.)

These likenesses are indeed striking, but have little bearing on our purpose of showing the relationship, if any, between the *character* of Seneca's *villain-heroes* and that of Shakespeare's. It is with Cunliffe's estimate of this influence that I disagree. He says, speaking of *Henry VI* and *Richard III*, " They are pervaded by the ruthless spirit of violence and bloodshed, and abound in the crude horrors of physical repulsiveness," but he quotes only examples from *Henry VI* to substantiate his charge. He then adds : " The murder of the young princes in *Richard III* is only narrated, and the executions in this play generally take place off the stage, only Clarence and

Richard himself dying in sight of the audience ; but the personages of the drama move in the same atmosphere of blood, and Richard above all sustains to the full his character of fiendish cruelty. He has the vindictiveness, the intellectual force, the undaunted spirit, the ruthless cruelty, the absolute lack of moral feeling of Seneca's Medea, coupled with the haughtiness of Eteocles, and the bloody hypocrisy of Atreus ; as with Seneca's heroic criminals, his passions know no bounds—he is not human but preternatural."

With this sweeping estimate of similarities in character I cannot agree. It is just because Richard is not like Seneca's villains in certain of these characteristics that the tragedy of *Richard III* is still actable and affects us profoundly, while Seneca's tragedies are artificial and repulsive.

In the first place the mere fact that all the murders but one, including the most distressing murder of the princes, take place off the stage makes all the difference in the world. It shows us that whereas Seneca is trying to impress us by shocking us, Shakespeare is trying to impress us with the power and mental qualities of the hero himself ; trying to get his tragic effect from character, not from spectacle. And he does this by removing from our sight those deeds resulting from the hero's commands which are simply shocking, and which by their own horrible fascination when seen or tellingly narrated would both draw away our attention from the finer psychological touches in character, and destroy our sympathy for the future progress of the hero. Moreover, though Richard is totally lacking in moral feeling, like Medea and Atreus, he does not exult in cruelty for its own sake as they do.   Richard is ruthless, indeed, but this cannot be attributed even to vindictiveness, for revenge is at no time his motive.   His end is absolute power, and to gain it he removes everyone that stands in his way.   So when his former accomplices desert him, as does Buckingham, he removes them too, but not so much because he is vindictive—i.e. seeking revenge for a personal injury—as because they are now new obstacles, and it is to his advantage to demonstrate the futility and danger of opposing him.   And to say that Richard is not human, but preternatural, is to miss the secret of the play's success.   It is just because he seems so human, though his human traits, good and bad, are developed far beyond the ordinary, that the play so grips us.   The Richard of the drama is no worse than the Richard of history, at least no worse than the Richard of history was and is supposed to have been, and what is believed to have been seems possible when imitated on the stage.[1]

Shakespeare, like Marlowe, emerges from Seneca's sickening atmosphere, but he excels Marlowe in keeping out of it.   Before the murder of the children Richard has our sympathy just as Barabas has— not the sympathy of pity, unless it be for his physical deformity, but sympathetic understanding.   For, admitting him tyrannical, what sort of men does he

[1] *History of the Life and Reign of Richard III*, by James Gairdner, Cam. Univer. Press, 1898.   In this historical monograph Dr. Gairdner reaches the conclusion that " the portrait with which we have been made familiar by Shakespeare and Sir Thomas More " is in all essential particulars faithful to the Richard of history.

practise upon ? We care little or nothing for the doom of " false, fleeting, perjured Clarence," and Hastings and Buckingham get no more than they have been giving others. Richard is no worse than his companions—simply bolder, and more energetic ; he remains free, as far as any pity for them is concerned, to hold our sympathy by what means he may. We felt this same indifference to the victims of the villain in the preceding tragedies, but were equally indifferent to the fate of the villain himself. The plays of which they are the heroes failed to arouse tragic emotion just as Aristotle foresaw. We found this to be due chiefly to lack of characterization or to absence of admirable qualities in the character of the hero. The plays depended for effect upon violent and spectacular means. Barabas, as long as he was psychologized, held our sympathy and admiration, but when he became a caricature and his deeds monstrous, all sympathy vanished and there was no element of pity or fear in our emotions at the end of the play. Now Richard, like Barabas, not only has bad qualities, but admirable qualities, and admirable in the highest degree ; and these characteristics are present in Richard until the very end. Barabas has an additional claim on our sympathies, however, because he has been outrageously injured, and this partly justifies his crimes. Sympathy arising from just provocation is even more prominent in the " revenge-for-a-father " type of play (to be later treated), because there revenge is treated as a convention which makes the act of the revenger a moral duty. But Richard has no such advantage ; ambition alone is his motive ; if he can

win us at all it must be by sheer force of character,
by the elements of greatness in his nature. We
might have had an opportunity to judge of the effects
of the combination of crime and greatness in Selimus
if that hero had only been vitalized, for Selimus
exhibits dauntless courage, ceaseless energy, and
able generalship, in addition to his villainous traits.
But he is little more than a personification of these
qualities, and so cannot be used as a convincing
example of the emotional effect of such characteristics upon the mind when portrayed in conjunction
with wickedness in what appears to us to be an
actual, living personality. In Richard we have such
a personality. He is wicked as well as great ; he is
a criminal and a villain, if there ever was one ; but
he is also human, and the play of which he is the hero
is a true tragedy. By what art does the dramatist
accomplish this result ?

Aristotle says that pity and fear are the only
tragic emotions, and that " pity is aroused by unmerited misfortune, fear by the misfortune of a man
like ourselves." Therefore, he argues, a villain
cannot arouse tragic emotion, because he merits
his misfortune and is unlike ourselves. We have
seen how sound this definition appeared when
applied to the tragedies hitherto considered ; but
experience teaches that *Richard III* does arouse
tragic emotion. The final effect has even something of the " katharsis " about it, for the play
does not leave us depressed or rebellious. It follows,
therefore, that either (1) pity and fear are not
the only tragic emotions, or (2) pity and fear may
be aroused by other means than the unmerited

misfortune of a man like ourselves ; or both (1) and
(2) may be true.

Aristotle's statement of the origin of fear—the
misfortune of a man like ourselves—is usually taken
to mean that when terrible events befall a good man
simply because of some error or frailty in his nature,
we, being likewise erring and frail, fear that something equally terrible might befall us in a similar
situation. When Othello, a man of passionate but
noble disposition, allows a jealous thought to take
root in his breast, it grows and spreads until it shuts
all light of love and reason from his nature. When
Lear in a moment of anger divides his kingdom
unjustly, a whole train of evil follows upon the
hasty and ill-considered act. When Hamlet hesitates instead of resolutely performing his duty, he
brings about the death of Polonius, Ophelia,
Laertes, and his own mother, as well as of himself.
Now, Othello, Lear, and Hamlet are all good men.
There are flaws in their natures, but such flaws
as might exist in any fine nature. We are all more
or less subject to jealousy ; anyone might act unjustly when his pride was piqued and his affections
wounded ; and anyone might hesitate to act because of self-doubt when action was most necessary.
We know that such frailty is a weakness of character,
but under ordinary circumstances no disastrous consequences would ensue. Only extraordinary conditions would make such weakness fatal. But how
can we foresee extraordinary circumstances ? How
can we tell when the results of our frailty will be
fatal ? We cannot. It is just this uncertainty and
the uncalculable nature of the terrible events that

may result from some error or frailty to which we are all subject that cause tragic fear. We must fear that we would do as the tragic heroes do and suffer as they suffer, under like circumstances, if it is *simply* the misfortune of a man like ourselves that rouses fear. Moreover, under such conditions we also pity the man who suffers, not because he deserves no punishment, but because he suffers beyond his deserts.

Now it goes without saying that Richard deserves all the punishment he receives. Hence, according to Aristotle's argument, we ought to feel no pity for him. And certainly he is not like ourselves ; we never feel for a moment that we could be guilty of such crimes as he commits. If there is one thing certain about Richard it is that he is *unlike* the ordinary man. It is his unusual gifts, as well as his unusual villainy, that render him such an absorbing figure. He is uncommon but not unnatural. The art of the poet preserves his humanity. According to the above theory, however, Richard should arouse neither pity nor fear. Hence, the emotion he inspired would not be tragic. But the conclusion reached by theory is contrary to our experience of fact. Richard actually does arouse deep emotion, and by the method of elimination, if by no other means, we could prove this emotion to be tragic. It is too profound for comedy ; it is not merely satisfaction ; and it is not disgust. What other name will describe it than tragic ? We are not reduced to the method of elimination, however. A close analysis of our emotions will show the presence of both pity and fear, and, in addition, the presence of other emotions proper to tragedy not considered by Aristotle.

All of these emotions, however, are roused in a manner different from that above described. We do not fear that we shall become like Richard, act like Richard, or suffer like him. What we do fear is Richard himself ; or, to put it another way, we fear the power of evil when embodied in a nature like Richard's. Fear in this instance does not arise from witnessing the misfortune of a man like ourselves, but from witnessing the consequences of power lodged in the hands of a man who is a villain, and who is totally unlike ourselves. The poet has taken pains to represent Richard as a gigantic, terror-inspiring figure. He is the absolute centre of the play ; everything is made dependent upon him ; he gives unity to the play itself ; " there is scarcely a thought, or feeling, or purpose expressed but what is either from him, or in some way concerning him, he being the author, the subject, or the occasion of it." [1] All his characteristics are exaggerated, but he seems real at the time. As he reveals himself in soliloquy he seems to be everything that he says he is—a man devoid of all the moral elements that restrain ordinary men; and gifted with the strength, the will, and the intellect to accomplish all that the most powerful man could accomplish when held in restraint by no moral scruples. Richard sets himself in defiance of morality, law, and order, and for a time appears to be successful in the contest. This it is which arouses our fear. Can it be that this terrible man with unlimited power and an

[1] H. N. Hudson, Preface to Aldus ed. of *Richard III*, p. xxxii.

atrophied conscience can go on and on and triumph over moral law and the natural order of things ? This is what Richard is doing, and he is so subtly characterized that it seems as though it were possible for a real man to do the like. This is the terror that Richard inspires, but it is allayed by his death. He is finally overcome, and overcome, so it seems, by divine justice, the moral order—Nemesis. He has been too forcibly impressed upon us for us to believe that any ordinary man or ordinary circumstances could overthrow him ; and the poet, to produce this impression, has had to make him too exclusively the centre of attraction to allow of the creation, by actual character study, of any equally great and human good force. Hence our fear is also for our faith in the omnipotence of a moral order, and it is the moral order, or Nemesis, that relieves our fear by defeating him. All critics have noticed the prevalence of the idea of Nemesis in this tragedy. This ethical note is not to be found in *The Jew of Malta*. To produce it, Shakespeare elaborates the counter-force, the force of righteousness in Richmond, by invoking God, by prophecies, by dreams and ghosts, and by the unaccountable heaviness that hangs over Richard's spirits, before the battle. Queen Margaret, also, whose presence in the drama flies in the face of history, is placed there for the very purpose of incarnating the idea of Nemesis, of divine justice. Simpson expresses very clearly the feeling we have for an external force :

" The play of *Richard III* exhibits the fate of virtuous weakness in the face of unscrupulous strength, and concludes with the fate of this strength in the face of providence. Henry VI perishes by natural causes. The forces which destroy Richard III are wholly supernatural . . . as if the lesson of the poet was that there is human remedy where there are ordinary human motives, but that for power joined with Machiavellian policy the only remedy is patience dependent on providence." [1]

Thus, then, we find that fear is present in the emotion aroused by this tragedy, and that it is " purged " by the triumph of Nemesis. Pity also is present, but in a lesser degree and in a peculiar form. It is not pity for the individual, as Aristotle suggests, but pity for the waste of great talents. For Richard, besides being the protagonist, the technical hero of the play, has many of the characteristics of the popular hero, the epic hero—" a man distinguished by extraordinary valour and martial achievements ; one who does brave deeds ; an illustrious warrior." [2] He is fearless, bold, and tremendously intellectual. These are great qualities which we cannot help admiring wherever found. Richard shows intellectual ability in all his tasks, whether in wooing Anne, or in handling his peers. Moreover, he enjoys his own intellectual combats, and that delights us and puts us even more in sympathy with him. As to his courage, the valour which he displays on the battlefield is but another side of that intrepidity which manifests itself in his defiance of law and conscience to win the throne single-handed. We do not admire the villain in him, but the great talents which he

[1] R. Simpson, *The Politics of Shakespeare's Historical Plays*, New Shak. Soc. Series, Vol. I, p. 424.
[2] *New Eng. Dict.*

turns to villainous ends. His audacity and demoniac
energy fascinate us ; our admiration is not willing,
but compelled. We sit spell-bound at the adroitness
with which he overcomes opposition and turns the
wickedness of others to his own advancement.
Power always fascinates ; and we have seen that
when we are conscious of the evil effects of its too
great abuse it may also inspire terror. It is equally
true, however, that when we see great and noble
talents neglected, or when we are deeply impressed
by the futility of their expenditure, we exclaim—
The pity of it, oh, the pity of it !

> Cut is the branch that might have grown full straight,
> And burned is Apollo's laurel bough,
> That sometime grew within this learned man.[1]

And yet the word pity, because we usually apply
the term to the individual, does not adequately
express the nature of the emotion aroused by the
tragedy of *Richard III*. Professor Bradley has used
the right word, I think, when he says that the loss
of much good in order to get rid of evil produces
upon the spectator an impression of " waste." We
believe in a moral order ; and in the tragic world
depicted by Shakespeare, this moral order is upheld.
But powers of evil are just as much in evidence,
though good triumphs in the end. All great tragedy
shows the weakness of man—his inability, no matter
how strong he is, to bring things to pass as he wishes,
to shape his own ends. The vain effort of man,
striving to shape his own ends, constitutes a tragic
struggle. There is, then, some ultimate power in
the tragic world against which man is powerless.

---

[1] Closing chorus of *Faustus*.

And the nature of this power is good. But at the
same time evil does exist. Hence, unless we believe
in dualism, we must acquiesce in the belief that the
ultimate power creates the evil as well as the good.
But the evil—to adopt another phrase of Professor
Bradley's—although self-generated, acts as "poison,"
and produces a convulsive struggle in the universe
to throw off this poison. It is finally cast out, but
at the expense of much good as well, and this
apparently inevitable loss of good along with evil
produces the impression of waste. The final effect
of such an impression is to create in us a feeling of
mystery and sadness, yet not depression, for the
good has prevailed.

This impression of waste is probably more marked
in *King Lear* than in any other tragedy, because in
it all the frightful forces of evil which destroy Lear
and Cordelia are let loose, not by crime on Lear's
part, but simply by one ill-advised, hot-headed,
selfish act—by error, in the true Aristotelian sense
of the word. Failure to conform to this ultimate
power which is making for perfection creates as
much havoc as an actual attack upon it ; error, or
ignorance (judging from results), is in itself a crime.
But when æsthetic good and ethical evil exist in the
same person, and when the destructive forces are
let loose by an actual attack on the moral order as
distinguished from failure to conform to it, the
sense of waste is not so great, because the sense of
justice crowds in and makes us feel that, though
possessed of great qualities which pass away with
him, the evil-doer should die.

Such is the case in *Richard III*. Nevertheless,

although we acknowledge the justice of the hero's fate, at the close of the tragedy we are conscious of waste even here. When we think of Richard the bold, Richard the versatile, Richard the intellectual giant having turned his talents and enormous energy —capable of so much good in the world—to evil ends resulting in his own death, we are saddened. For we are forced to admire ability so far above our own, and we cannot but feel sorrowful and mysteriously impressed when it is so used as to counteract itself, so as to be finally blotted out, leaving no trace of itself.

It must be admitted that *Richard III* arouses at different stages of the action admiration, terror, and sadness, and that owing to the violence of the struggle and the magnitude of the forces involved we feel even awe. Now, these emotions are tragic ; they are even more tragic than pity and fear, for they include them. Aristotle's definition is not quite comprehensive enough for a tragedy like *Richard III*. He mentions only such pity as is felt for the individual and such fear as is aroused by the individual's misfortune. His theory does not embrace the sadness produced by the sense of waste, nor the terror inspired by the acts of the individual ; nor does he consider the fact that a villain, while totally devoid of qualities that are good in the moral sense, may possess qualities that are æsthetically good—i.e. admirable, great—and that these characteristics when highly developed and combined with an evil nature may be brought into collision with moral law in such a way as to produce the tragic emotion of awe. Inducing his theory as he did, however, simply

from the Greek tragedies before him, the marvel is
that, with the exception of one or two of Shakespeare's plays, his theory should prove to be universally applicable.

And even though we insist that *Richard III* is
tragic, we must admit that fear rather than pathos
predominates. The prevalence of fear may be
ascribed to two causes. In the first place Richard
does not simply waste his strength ; he misuses it
so frightfully as to leave us little time to think what
good things *might* be done with it, in our realization
of the terrible things that *are being* done. The real
sense of waste does not come until Richard is killed
and all his efforts are shown to have been futile ;
for while he is active, fear and admiration alternate.

Besides, Richard is on one occasion needlessly
cruel. The murder of the children in the Tower is
committed without political necessity, and is heinous
beyond all his other tyrannous acts combined. It
is, in fact, his one unforgivable crime.[1] This brings

---

[1] This seems to have been likewise the case in history. " The
disorders of civil war had accustomed the nation to see justice
sometimes executed without the due formalities ; and his neglect
of those formalities had not hitherto made him unpopular.
But . . . the news (of the murder of the Princes), once made
public, ran like wildfire through the country, and was received
with groans and indignation in every street and market-place.
. . . The intelligence (of the disaffection) evidently took the
king quite by surprise. He was in the midst of his Northern
progress, enjoying every evidence of devoted loyalty and of
his own personal popularity. If, notwithstanding these demon-
strations, he was conscious of one dreadful fact calculated to
turn against him the hearts of the people, he seems to have been
singularly ill-prepared for the consequences. He had not even
the Great Seal with him, and had no means of calling adherents
to his aid." Gairdner (supra), p. 129 ff. Surely this is sufficient
testimony that the people over whom he ruled had given no
evidence of hating him.

out the element in Richard's character which makes
him an absolute villain. We have already noted
that there must be elements of greatness in a
character to make him a sympathetic protagonist.
To make him a villain, wilfulness is of equal importance. Crime is crime as far as punishment is concerned, but if wilfulness is not distinctly manifest
we can sympathize with the criminal. If fate or
necessity shows up more than wilfulness we can see
ourselves in his place. He is representative of us :
he could not help himself. Every man's will is his
own, but his frailty and susceptibility to error are
part of us. A man like Œdipus has our sympathy
entirely, because his crime was committed in ignorance ; he is not a villain at all. Villainy *includes*
the idea of wilfulness, and, in a tragedy properly
motivated, where cause and effect hang together,
the villain's overthrow is due to wilfulness. The
more wilful a man is the more difficult it is to sympathize with him. And here we find the reason for
our lack of pity for Richard. In him wilfulness is
not modified but accentuated. He never hesitates,
never feels remorse ; his character undergoes no
change or development ; he is a villain first and last.
Disintegration is suggested only once, and then in
the third scene of the last act, where the ghosts of
his victims appear in his sleep. His waking language,
however, which results from his dreams, is much
more impressive than the visualization of the dream
itself through the ghosts. In his soliloquy he shows
what a terrible strain the suppression of his conscience has cost him. For a moment he lives in fear
and dejection even while awake. But this scene

comes too late, and is not sufficient, alone, to awaken sympathy for any internal struggle. Our interest soon returns to its former centre in the hero's energy and courage. The ghost scene impresses us rather with the fact that there is an unseen power of good working to counteract Richard's visible evil deeds, and suggests that its force is acting retributively on him in his sleep when he no longer controls his reasoning powers. It suggests mystery, but it does not produce an abiding impression that Richard has constantly a war going on within himself. This is the chief difference between *Richard III* and *Macbeth*. This technical imperfection—lack of character development—combines with wilfulness to make *Richard III* the inferior tragedy of the two.

Richard's villainy is so dire, his wilfulness is so great, that at times it almost alienates us. But he is too great a man, the struggle in which he engages is too magnificent to permit of any such result. We are forced to admit that, in spite of the fact that the hero of *Richard III* is a villain, the play far surpasses in tragic effect anything presented before it, and deserves to be ranked among great tragedies. " We must not demand of Tragedy any and every kind of pleasure, but only that which is proper to it." [1] True, and the pre-Shakespearean villains create only a sense of the monstrous, or at best satisfy our sense of justice, without producing real tragic pleasure. But *Richard III* actually does create such pleasure, and by means " proper " to tragedy, namely, mystery, sadness, and awe. But the mix-

[1] Aristotle's *Poetics* (supra), p. 49

ture is not in the right proportion. Hence, although
we agree that *Richard III* is a great tragedy, we
must also admit that it is not of the first order, that
it is not one of the greatest. No one would class it,
for instance, with *Macbeth, Hamlet, King Lear,* or
Othello. It rises above what Aristotle calls the
Second Rank—those tragedies which have a double
thread of plot and an opposite catastrophe for the
good and the bad (like *The Merchant of Venice*), the
pleasure arising from which, he says, is proper to
comedy ; but it does not rise to the very highest
rank of those tragedies whose emotional effect is so
great and purifying that we leave them in a state of
exaltation.

VIII

THE REVENGEFUL VILLAIN-HERO

A NUMBER of years elapsed before the ambitious villain again appeared upon the stage in the plays of Shakespeare and Jonson, but in the meantime villains of another type were constantly before the public—villains whose leading motive was not ambition, but revenge. Most of these villains are also Machiavellians, for ambition is not the *sine qua non* of Machiavellism. It does not make so much difference what the direct cause of action may be, provided the actions themselves, the methods adopted to attain the sought-for end, reveal the typical Machiavellian characteristics. In many cases ambition and revenge are blended, as in Barabas, but even then one or the other usually predominates sufficiently to enable us to designate it as the leading motive.

The plays of Kyd and Marlowe have again to be considered in connection with this new element, for in one respect or another the great majority of later villain-heroes were affected by the types established by the heroes of *The Spanish Tragedy* and *The Jew of Malta*. From Seneca, Kyd took over the ghost, the motive of revenge, and soliloquy, as well as various other motives of interest in the

99

study of the drama as a whole. In Seneca the desire
for revenge is somewhat excusable, as it rises either
from gross ingratitude and faithlessness, as in
Medea, or from the murder of a relative or the
corruption of a wife or a mother, as in *Agamemnon*
and *Thyestes*. As we have seen, however, these
motives are not sufficient to overcome the malice
and exultation in suffering which make the avenger
a villain. In *The Spanish Tragedy*, however, Kyd
transforms revenge into a convention, and justifies
it. It is undertaken by a father for the wanton
murder of a son ; no other redress for the injury
is possible ; the avenger feels that revenge is a
solemn duty, yet vacillates from doubt ; while a
ghost and the spirit of Revenge, as emissaries of
the gods of the under-world, act as a chorus and
thus heighten the sense of revenge as a sacred duty.
Consequently Hieronimo is no villain. But Lorenzo,
against whom Hieronimo is working for the murder
of his son, is. Yet he too is an avenger. In this
one play we have two types of revenge : that of
Hieronimo the hero, and that of Lorenzo the villain.
We have already seen that this Lorenzo, though a
secondary figure in *The Spanish Tragedy*, was very
important because of his Machiavellian traits. He
is just as important on account of the spirit of
revenge which animates him. Kyd, by creating
Hieronimo, actually established a type for one kind
of avenging hero ; Marlowe established another
type by supplying his hero Barabas with the motives
of revenge that animate Kyd's villain. As prototype of Barabas, Lorenzo is all-important. Not
only are the character and actions of these two

villains alike, but the motive for their first crime is
in each case revenge—a revenge, however, to be
sharply distinguished in nature from that of Hieronimo. In the case of Kyd's villain and of Marlowe's
hero, revenge is a criminal passion ; in the case of
Kyd's hero, it is a sacred duty. Lorenzo kills
Horatio (Hieronimo's son) from personal animosity ;
his motive can hardly be dignified by the term
revenge. He is jealous of the honours bestowed
upon Horatio for bravery, and is incensed because
Horatio, as accepted suitor, stands in the way of a
match which he proposes for his sister, Bellimperia.
The motive for the murder of Horatio is thus seen
to have been entirely personal and unjustifiable.
Now it was this personal element—which one
expects in a villain, but condemns—that Marlowe
took over and imparted to his hero. And Barabas,
we know, is the father of a numerous progeny of
villain-heroes. He is ambitious and a Machiavellian,
and a long line of Machiavellian villains whose sole
motive is ambition follows in his train. But ambition is not the instigating cause of his criminal
actions ; revenge is the motive. Revenge in his
case is more justifiable, it is true, than in the case
of Lorenzo, for the latter has no higher motives
than envy and selfishness to vindicate his actions ;
while Barabas suffers a great wrong for which,
moreover, he can expect no redress except such as
he can bring about by his own actions. But palliate
his vindictiveness as we may, the revenge of Barabas
is not the justifiable revenge of Kyd's hero. It is
not for the murder of a son or a father ; nor is it
a solemn duty ; nor directed against a single

individual as in the case of Hieronimo and Hamlet. Although we sympathize with Barabas on account of the greatness of his character and the extent of his wrongs, we nevertheless regard him as a villain, because his revenge is criminal. But we do not regard Hieronimo as a villain. The distinction to be borne in mind is that the Machiavellian type of avenger is moved to revenge by personal resentment and desire for retaliation, whether the occasion for resentment be great or small ; whereas revenge of the type that marks Kyd's heroes is more or less of a sacred nature, always obligatory, and is justified as a code. The result is that the Machiavellian type of avenger is always a villain, though sometimes the hero, whereas the revenger modelled on Hieronimo or Hamlet is always the hero, but never a villain unless the dramatist fails to justify the code of revenge.

In addition to this primary distinction the Marlowean villain, as the succeeding analyses of all plays representing such a type will show, has no regard whatever for human beings, but sweeps them away as though they were so many flies. Although we nowhere find in Machiavelli's *bona fide* writings such an attitude toward human life supported, the attitude probably came to be regarded as Machiavellian because of Gentillet's numerous maxims counselling infidelity and cruelty, as well because Barabas—who was regarded as a typical Machiavellian—attempts to kill men in such a wholesale fashion in the last three acts.

Examples of Machiavellian villainy resulting from revenge of the sort typified by Barabas are

Aaron in *Titus Andronicus,* Eleazar in *Lust's Dominion,* and (with certain modifications) Iago. But added to their Machiavellian traits is malignity —a Senecan motive not used by Kyd and Marlowe— a spirit delighting not only in successful revenge or superior cunning, but in seeing the victim suffer.

Descended from the " revenge-for-a-father " type of play, originated by Kyd, are *Antonio's Revenge, Hoffmann, Revenger's Tragedy,* and *The Atheist's Tragedy.* This is not to say, however, that the heroes of these plays resemble the hero of *The Spanish Tragedy.* Hoffmann, indeed, is the old avenger for the death of a father, but in this instance that avenger has degenerated into a villain. Piero (*Antonio's Revenge*) is the villain, like Lorenzo, against whom the justified avenger aims. He is also lustful, which almost puts him in a class by himself ; and likewise politically ambitious, which connects him with the line descending from Selimus. In addition, he, like Aaron, exults in suffering. In fact, Piero represents a very mixed type, but from him, rather than from Barabas or Aaron, descend Hoffmann, Vendici, and Bosola of Webster's *Duchess of Malfi.*

Titus Andronicus (written before 1594) shows the influence of both *The Spanish Tragedy* and *The Jew of Malta.* The revenge of Titus for his children, his feigned madness but really distraught condition, the sub-plot of intrigue managed by Aaron, whose machinations are the cause of Titus' revenge, all remind one of *The Spanish Tragedy,* while the character of Aaron and the nature of his deviltry show the influence of Barabas. Titus is the real

hero, and is qualified to come within Aristotle's
definition of a great man, as one fundamentally
good, of high rank, and famous. His tragic error
lies in condemning the son of Tamora to death.
This cannot be regarded as a crime, however, as it
was done as a religious duty and with no sense of
wrong. Titus actually becomes a criminal like
Atreus when he slays Tamora's sons, but he is
instantly killed, and his death ends the play ; but
during the time he holds our attention as hero, he
is a man rather sinned against than sinning.

Technically, I presume, the fiendish revenge of
Tamora would be called the sub-plot, and Tamora
the protagonist. As a matter of fact, however,
Aaron directs the entire action and she falls in with
his plots. It is his villainy, moreover, that gives
colour to the whole tragedy. As one of the Romans
states in the final scene, it is

> this execrable wretch,
> That hath been breeder of these dire events.

Or, as he himself says (V, i) in speaking of the crimes
of Tamora's sons :

> Indeed, I was their tutor to instruct them :
>
> .   .   .   .   .
>
> That bloody mind, I think, they learn'd of me.

In all probability the figure of the Moor remains
longer and more vividly in the memory of the aver-
age reader than that of any other personage in the
tragedy.

Except that he does not use poison, Aaron shows
all the worst traits of a Machiavellian villain. He
makes use of the viciousness of other men to serve

his own turns; he counsels others to the most atrocious crimes; he does not hesitate at murder, but slays with his own hands the nurse who is a witness to his criminal intercourse with Tamora; he is a cynic, an egotist, and an atheist. His atheism (if any doubt as to its existence remains) is established by his own admission in the scene where he promises to reveal all he knows if Lucius will swear to save his child :

> *Aar.* Swear that he shall, and then I will begin.
> *Luc.* Who should I swear by ? thou believest no god :
> That granted, how canst thou believe an oath ?
> *Aar.* What if I do not ? As, indeed, I do not.

Like Barabas, he dies unrepentant :

> O, why should wrath be mute, and fury dumb ?
> I am no baby, I, that with base prayers
> I should repent the evils I have done :
> Ten thousand worse than ever yet I did
> Would I perform, if I might have my will .
> If one good deed in all my life I did,
> I do repent it from my very soul.

During his lifetime he is guileful and deceitful ; it is the intrigue resulting from his craftiness which enlivens the action. Some critics have accused him of lust, but his character is not debased by this un-Machiavellian vice. That he has no moral scruples goes without saying, but he is no slave to lust ; his passions are well under control, as is clear from the fact that he never gives way to lustful speech as do the sons of Tamora, and that he resists the importunities of Tamora herself, saying :

> Madam, though Venus govern your desires,
> Saturn is dominator over mine :
> What signifies my deadly-standing eye,
> My silence and my cloudy melancholy

> My fleece of woolly hair that now uncurls
> Even as an adder when she doth unroll
> To do some fatal execution ?
> No, madam, these are no venereal signs :
> Vengeance is in my heart, death in my hand,
> Blood and revenge are hammering in my head.
>
> (II, iii, 30–9.)

He only makes use of the lust of others to further his own ends. This is true whether in the case of the lust of the sons of the queen for Lavinia, or in the case of the queen's lust for himself :

> Now climbeth Tamora Olympus' top,
> Safe out of fortune's shot, and sits aloft,
> Secure of thunder's crack or lightning flash,
> Advanced above pale envy's threatening reach.
>
> . . . . .
>
> Upon her wit doth earthly honour wait,
> And virtue stoops and trembles at her frown.
> Then, Aaron, arm thy heart, and fit thy thoughts,
> To mount aloft with thy imperial mistress,
> And mount her pitch, whom thou in triumph long
> Hast prisoner held, fetter'd in amorous chains,
> And faster bound to Aaron's charming eyes
> Than is Prometheus tied to Caucasus.   (II, i.)

Not lust, but revenge is the passion that Aaron seeks to gratify :

> Vengeance is in my heart, death in my hand,
> Blood and revenge are hammering in my head.
>
> (Supra.)

His revenge, moreover, is utterly unjustifiable ; it bears no relation whatever to that of Hieronimo or Hamlet, but does resemble that of Barabas. Barabas, however, had at first an understandable motive for his revenge which Aaron has not. It is true that Aaron belongs to a subjected nation, but this hardly explains either his hatred of the whole human race,

or the depth of his malice, for deep malignity seems
to have been always a part of his nature. He portrays himself, just as Barabas does (and with greater
verisimilitude), as a monster who all his life has
exulted in the misfortune of others :

> Even now I curse the day—and yet, I think,
> Few come within the compass of my curse—
> Wherein I did not some notorious ill :
> As kill a man, or else devise his death ;
> Ravish a maid, or plot the way to do it ;
> Accuse some innocent, and forswear myself ;
> Set deadly enmity between two friends ;
> Make poor men's cattle break their necks ;
> Set fire on barns and hay-stacks in the night,
> And bid the owners quench them with their tears.
> Oft have I digged up dead men from their graves,
> And set them upright at their dear friends' doors,
> Even when their sorrows almost were forgot ;
> And on their skins, as on the bark of trees,
> Have with my knife carved with Roman letters
> ' Let not your sorrow die though I am dead.'
> Tut, I have done a thousand dreadful things
> As willingly as one would kill a fly ;
> And nothing grieves me heartily indeed,
> But that I cannot do ten thousand more. (V, i, 125.)

The triumph of guileful wickedness over innocent
simplicity is portrayed in nearly all villain-hero
plays, and the doctrine that success is to be attained
through such means came to be regarded as Machiavellian, just as though it were the same thing as
political policy. This was partly due to Gentillet's
abuse, partly, perhaps, to Marlowe himself. To
understand the nature of a person who acts upon
such a theory it is necessary to imagine the feelings
of a man of excessive self-confidence, an egotist,
who believes that he is much more capable than
those around him, disbelieves entirely in the

profession of unselfishness on the part of others, but finds himself so cramped by circumstances that he is unable to exhibit his powers through ordinary channels. Inwardly raging at his helplessness, and envious of those in power, he finds the only outlet for his consuming energy in crime, and satisfies his vanity by marring the lives and happiness of those who think they are his masters and superiors. Some such assumption might explain Aaron's desire to exercise his ingenuity at the expense of those in authority, but it does not explain his treatment of Titus, who is in very ill-favour. Moreover, it does not explain his joy in evil for evil's sake, as opposed to joy in evil as the exemplification of successful policy. Nor does it explain his devilish delight in mutilation—physical suffering—his satisfaction in cutting off the hand of Titus, for example.

> I play'd the cheater for thy father's hand ;
> And, when I had it, drew myself apart,
> And almost broke my heart with extreme laughter :
> I pried me through the crevice of a wall
> When for his hand he had his two sons' heads ;
> Beheld his tears and laugh'd so heartily
> That both mine eyes were raining like to his.

This is more after the manner of Atreus exulting in the suffering of Thyestes. It is not to be found in *The Jew of Malta*. But the long passage quoted, beginning " Even now I curse the day," enumerating all the wickedness of his past life, is not Senecan at all. It was taken undoubtedly from the similar utterance by Barabas. When Barabas speaks his lines they are not in keeping with his character, but the latter part of his career seems to be given

over to an endeavour to make them prophetic.
However, such a career as that pictured in Aaron's
speech is simply monstrous. It expresses malignity,
to be sure, but absolutely motiveless malignity.
It does not carry the shudder with it that his actual
deeds do. Such malignity is unreal—

> The venomous malice of (a) swelling heart—

portrayed by the dramatist for theatrical effect
without regard to probability.

We find, then, that Aaron is a Machiavellian,
that he resembles Barabas in boasting of the horror
and number of his past crimes, and that his revenge
is unjustifiable. We find in addition that much of
his malignity is motiveless, and that the pleasure
he takes in contemplating suffering resembles
nothing so much as the brutal joy of Seneca's
villain-heroes. To relieve the blackness of his
character the poet endows Aaron with courage,
love for his child, an acid humour, and an intellectuality which, though not great, is superior to that of
his associates. These qualities, however, are not
sufficiently developed to arouse any sympathy.
Were the Moor the technical hero, therefore, the
tragedy would be a failure. Nevertheless, though
Aaron is simply a villain, and an unsympathetic
villain at that, he established a type which lasted
until a late date.

In *Lust's Dominion* we have the Aaron type
pushed forward as protagonist in the person of
Eleazar. Although there is some evidence for
identifying this play with *The Spanish Moor's
Tragedy*, a work in which Dekker, Haughton, and

Day combined in 1600,[1] the resemblance to *Titus
Andronicus* is so strong in the two lascivious
queens, the two Moors, the accumulation of horrors,
and the crudeness of the work, that it seems almost
certain that it was conceived, whether written in
its present form or not, in the early nineties.[2]

Eleazar is distinctly the central figure, and con-
trives the major portion of the action.   He is a
Moorish prince subjected by the king of Spain.
He commences his tragic career moved by revenge
and hatred for the whole Spanish race, and advances
continuously to success by committing atrocious
crimes until the final act, when he is finally caught
in his own trap and overthrown.   The lust of the
queen-mother for Eleazar gives him a fulcrum upon
which to get a purchase for removing those who
are personally hateful to him, as well as those who
stand in the way of his advancement.   In one of his
soliloquies he thus coolly foredooms the whole
Spanish court :

> Let's see now, by her falling I must rise;
> Cardinal, you die if the king bid me live ;
> Philip, you die for railing at me ;
> Proud lord, you die, that with Mendoza cried,
> Banish the Moor.
> And you, my loving liege, you're best sit fast :
> If all these live not, you must die at last.
>
> (End of Act I.)

The manner in which he profits by the wickedness
of others to advance himself is very much like that

---

[1] Cf. Collier in his edition of Henslowe, 165. See also Collier's
Shakespeare, 1853, iv, 98, for the mention of a " tract upon
which some of the scenes [of this tragedy] are even verbally
founded."

[2] Cf. Fleay, i, 272.

of Barabas, Aaron, and Richard III. He uses the queen's influence to banish the Cardinal, Mendoza, who has made himself hateful to the Moor ; he uses the lust of King Ferdinand for Maria (Eleazar's wife) as an excuse to murder him ; he then uses the queen's lust again to proclaim her second son Philip a bastard and thus shut him off from the throne ; he imprisons the Infanta's husband and tries to win her love in order to entrench himself in power by making his actual power also legal. But here he runs against a stumbling-block. She remains chaste, and her beauty so affects one of the Moor's slaves that he frees her husband and Philip, who, disguised as slaves themselves, trap and execute Eleazar. The play is long-drawn-out and repulsive, but the threads of influence are closely interwoven. Given the wily, lustful characters of the persons of the drama, the events follow fairly consistently as cause and effect until the last act, when the betrayal of his master by the guard is unreasonable. Eleazar advances to success by means of his policy, his boldness, and the weakness of those with whom he deals ; to overthrow him the *deus ex machina* has to be introduced. The outline of the plot might suggest the situation presented in *Richard III*—viz. the fate of virtuous weakness in the face of unscrupulous strength—but the play itself suggests no such problem, owing to feeble characterization.

Machiavellian policy guides the actions of the hero. Eleazar does not get rid of any of his enemies by himself using poison, but he suggests its use to his wife. Neither is he found quoting Machiavellian

maxims, but the principles that govern his conduct
are so evident that they need no such tag. He
nowhere says that it is better to be feared than
loved, for instance, but his actions show that such
is his conviction. The following aphoristic statement illustrates the principle well enough, though
it modifies the language :

> *Ele.*   The bitterness shall be wash'd off with blood :
> Tyrants swim safest in a crimson flood.   (V, iii.)

He rids himself of such accomplices as the friars,
who can no longer assist him, upon the principle that

> Slaves too much trusted do grow dangerous.   (II, v.)

This aphorism recalls Lorenzo and Barabas, and
certain maxims of Gentillet.[1]

He is an egotist, and trusts no one but himself.
As he stands rapt, plotting the future destruction
of his enemies, the queen begs his confidence. He
is about to give it, but refrains :

> Why, thus ; yet, no :—let's hence,
> My heart is nearest to my council.   (IV, iv.)

Though he profits by the lust of others he never
lets lust get the upper hand of himself.

He himself murders the king, but as a rule prefers
to make others his tools for risky and criminal acts.
After he has been proclaimed king, however, and
when he thinks he is firmly fixed in his place, he
plans such a wholesale murder of the former rulers
of the country as can only be compared with
Barabas' attempt to massacre all the Turks.

In policy he is more of a fox than a lion, but is so

---

[1] Gentillet, I, 3 ; III, 10, 20, 21.

situated that he needs to be ; the qualities of the latter are not wanting in him, as may be seen from his courage in battle.

He says nothing about religion, and does not use it as a cloak to crime, in this respect differing from Barabas ; but that he is devoid of religion is evident from his actions. He is frequently called a devil by other persons in the play, and he dies cursing, as did Barabas.

He is not portrayed as rich or usurious, but certainly in his case wealth was to be obtained by his policy, for he practically controlled the purse strings through the queen. This is the Machiavellian policy of which Patericke accuses French courtiers.[1]

His ambition for the throne of Spain and his use of craft to obtain it are both Machiavellian. But this ambition is not pressed constantly to the front as in the Selimus type. Eleazar belongs rather to that other Machiavellian type who is spurred to action by revenge and general hatred, but who feels ambition and takes a cunning delight in manifesting his power by secret artifice ; who takes a cynical enjoyment in watching wickedness and guile triumph over benevolent authority. Malignity may be called a motive, if we mean by motive a cause for action, and in this sense malignity is Eleazar's motive as it is Aaron's. But when we come to look for a dramatic cause for the malignity itself, it is even more wanting in the case of Eleazar than of Aaron. For, though Eleazar is a conquered prince, he is in high favour, and practically governs

---

[1] Cf. Dedicatory letter in Patericke.

his conquerors through his influence with the queen ;
and no motive of excessive Moorish patriotism is
put forward to convince us that, in spite of his own
power, love of country still swells his hatred against
the dominant race. This far-reaching malignity of
a cynical egotist is what differentiates this particular type of Machiavellian villain.

On the other hand, the fiendish joy which Eleazar
takes in tormenting his victims is reminiscent of
Seneca's Thyestes and Medea, rather than of
Machiavelli, and is only found in Aaron, Eleazar,
Piero, Vendici, and, with certain modifications,
Iago. The typical Machiavellian is willing to commit
any crime to gain his end, whether that end be the
gratification of ambition or revenge ; he may even
rejoice in his power and success ; but it is the
Senecan villain that takes his greatest pleasure in
the suffering itself.

On account of this repulsive trait the Moor does
not at any point arouse our admiration. His only
admirable trait is courage, and that is neither so
great nor so frequently exercised as to counteract
in any way the effect of his wickedness. His downfall does not arouse our pity, because he deserves
it. He does not inspire terror like Richard (or even
Iago), for his plots show no remarkable intellectual
power, and nearly all with whom he deals are base ;
it is lust's dominion, and, except for Philip and
Isabella, it would make little difference whether
his deviltry were successful or not. The play does
not really touch our deep emotions, because none
of the characters is real enough or great enough to
call forth such fundamental feelings as love, hatred,

pity, or fear. Soliloquy is used, as is usual in villain-hero plays, to acquaint us with the designs of the hero. But even with the aid of this device, Eleazar does not arouse our sympathy. The reason for this is that there is nothing noble about his ambition, and, being in high favour, he cannot very well awaken pity or sympathy by dwelling on the humility of his position as a captive. The only effect of the soliloquies is to emphasize his position as protagonist, by centring our attention on the plots which he conceives and attempts to carry through. But his character never develops : he is the same cruel monster from beginning to end. For these reasons he touches no single sympathetic chord in our hearts, and his fall into adversity leaves no tragic impression.

Iago is the Aaron type of villain humanized. He is egotistical, guileful, cruel, faithless, remorseless, cynical, and murderous ; he also uses one man to destroy another, and then slays his accomplice. All of these traits we have found in every villain whom we have classed as a Machiavellian. In addition, Iago bears a striking, though superficial, resemblance to Aaron and Eleazar in the particular characteristics which those villains possess over and above their distinctly Machiavellian traits. In the first place, the term " motiveless malignity " which we have appropriated to express the virulent animosity of Aaron and Eleazar was first applied by Coleridge to the ill-will of Iago. In the second place, Iago takes pleasure in the suffering of his victim in much the same manner, apparently, as Seneca's villains, from whom Aaron and Eleazar derive this trait. But, whereas they are unconvincing, melodramatic stage villains, Iago is terribly real. His lifelikeness is proved beyond a doubt by the hatred every reader and spectator bears him ; he could not arouse such intense feeling unless we believed in his reality.

Shakespeare was evidently profoundly impressed by the wickedness in the world, and has left us the immortal fruit of his study of the conflict between good and evil in their most far-reaching aspects in *King Lear* and *Macbeth*. In *Richard III* he portrayed a tyrant dominated by evil principles, and a tyrant in every respect a Machiavellian prince. As he turned his hand to practically every type of drama current in his day and perfected it— comedy, chronicle play, romantic love, the revenge type in Hamlet, the political villain in Richard— it seems not improbable that in his musings over wickedness he was influenced to accept the story in Cynthio's Novels as a working basis to portray such evil as we find in Iago, because of the frequent appearance on the stage of such villains as Aaron, Eleazar, Piero, Hoffmann, and others who are remarkable for their depravity and delight in outwitting and tormenting the innocent and guileless. Such stage characters must have appeared very crude to an intellect like Shakespeare's, yet the poet could not but recognize that individuals with hard hearts and busy brains, with apparently no social feeling, no goodwill for their fellows, do exist, and he set himself to portray such an individual, to exhibit the workings of his mind—its activity as well as its shortcomings—in Iago.

Now Iago is as much the hero of the tragedy of *Othello* as is Othello himself. It is a play with two protagonists, the one sympathetic, the other repulsive. It is Othello whom we admire and pity ; his suffering it is which arouses tragic emotion. He is the great man whose fall through error and frailty awakens pity and fear. But Iago is nevertheless a protagonist, and his tragedy is just as much in evidence as Othello's, though we have no pity for him. *Othello* is a drama of intrigue as well as of character, and Iago is the intriguer. It is Iago's plot which sets the action in motion ; it is his inexhaustible resources and indefatigable energy which keeps it going. He is not the kind of villain who blocks the hero's purpose ; he creates a purpose for Othello. It is the poison which he pours into Othello's mind which drives Othello to action, and this is in itself part of Iago's purpose. And just as Othello's fall is the result of a flaw in his character—an ungovernable passion, and too great a susceptibility to deceit, a trust in the nobility of man's nature not warranted by general experience—so Iago's fall is brought about by the very opposite flaw—an insufficient insight into the power of lofty and altruistic ideals.

If we acknowledge, however, that Iago, though bearing the stamp of the type-villain, is made human and effective, it becomes necessary to point out how the psychologizing process is brought about. Shakespeare attains verisimilitude in the first instance by doing away with practically all bombast. Though the presence of the distinguishing characteristics of the type stamp Iago as a Machiavel-

lian, the very absence of certain other features,
melodramatic in nature, which are usually associated with Machiavellism, proclaims his humanness.
He is not a butcher, for instance ; he does not kill
men like flies ; he does not boast of slaying his
accomplice as though boasting were his rôle ; he
does not die cursing, which is melodramatic, but
dies stubbornly, stoically, which is tragic. As a
result, we have left not a monstrosity, or a caricature, but a man, whose villainy is infinitely more
terrifying because of its reality.

Secondly, although Iago takes a malicious delight
in tormenting Othello, it is because he hates the
Moor for what he considers a personal affront, and
because his suffering is an indication of the successful issue of Iago's guileful policy. It is not physical
agony that pleases him ; nothing could be further
from the exultation born of pride which marks
Iago than the exultation born of pure malice which
marks Aaron and Eleazar. Their malice is universal,
inhuman, and inexplicable ; his is limited to particular individuals, and has a motive. He manifests no pleasure whatever in being near Desdemona while she suffers, and he even hesitates about
killing Roderigo and Cassio. He decides, indeed,
to do so because it is evident that it is better for his
safety to have them out of the way, but he takes no
wanton joy in it.

> *Iago.*   Now whether he [Roderigo] kill Cassio,
> Or Cassio him, or each do kill the other,
> Every way makes my gain : live Roderigo,
> He calls me to a restitution large
> Of gold and jewels that I bobb'd from him,
> As gifts to Desdemona :

It must not be : if Cassio do remain,
He hath a daily beauty in his life
That makes me ugly ; and besides, the Moor
May unfold me to him ; there stand I in much peril :
No, he must die. Be't so. I hear him coming.

Moreover, the term " motiveless malignity,"
which is appropriate in the case of Aaron and
Eleazar, is, as a matter of fact, not at all applicable
to Iago. He has four motives for his conduct :
suspicion of Othello's relation with Emilia ; desire
to gain Cassio's place ; hatred of Othello for failing to recognize the talents which Iago sees in
himself ; and an overmastering desire to justify his
own egotistical principles by seeing his own will
and intellectual astuteness triumph over those who
think themselves and are regarded by others as
good. Of these motives the last is by far the most
important, and involves the other three. Iago has
a certain kind of ambition, but it is not of the same
nature as that of Selimus and Richard III. The
desire for Cassio's place, though a motive, is not
strong enough in itself to have driven Iago to
action. The desire to display his own skill and to
prove the efficacy of his egotistical principles is
his real ambition. But this motive is so inextric-
ably interwoven with and dependent upon the motive
of hatred that Iago can by no means be classed
with the type of villain termed ambitious. His
pride has been injured by his intellectual inferiors,
and he consequently seeks a revenge that will
restore his pride and justify his egotism. Revenge
is thus seen to be the impelling motive, though it
partakes of the nature of ambition.

Owing to the fact that Iago does not harp upon

the motives for his action, but takes them up simply to dismiss them, as it were, the three minor motives above-mentioned, though usually considered by critics, have been regarded as insufficient to account for Iago's villainy, and have, therefore, been regarded as mere instances of " motive hunting " ; whereas the fourth motive, the Machiavellian motive, which explains and lends strength to the other three, has been too frequently ignored.   It has been stated, for instance, that Iago's desire for Cassio's office is but feigned, and that he has no cause for hating Othello.   Now, although Iago is a liar, there is no reason for accepting his words at other than their face value when he has no motive for lying, or when the audience is not in a position either to suspect the lie or detect it immediately afterwards.   Thus in the opening scene between Roderigo and Iago, the latter says that he hates Othello for having chosen Cassio instead of himself as lieutenant.   The speech has the ring of envy and contempt, and really expresses Iago's character. No one will believe that Othello dismissed the " three great ones of the city," who preferred Iago's suit, with " bombast circumstance " ;   the description does not fit Othello.   But there is no reason to doubt that Iago did apply for the position, and it is perfectly natural that a disappointed suitor should so describe his refusal.   Again, no one will judge Cassio by Iago's contemptuous description of him, for the words issue from the mouth of a disappointed rival, and at once suggest that the disparagement is unjust.   But the evident disappointment which the words reveal proves that

Iago wanted the office. Moreover, his language is such as to leave no doubt that he not only resented the loss of the office, but also hated the holder thereof. His irritation is that of a man who " knows his price " and is angry that other people do not. Iago is no commonplace grumbler, no dull-witted office seeker envious of everyone above him ; but he is nevertheless subject to vexation and anger when the merit which he sees in himself is passed by unrecognized. He seeks promotion, presumably for the same reasons that would actuate anyone else, but the mortification, resentment, and rankling desire for revenge that follow upon his disappointment are peculiar to himself.

This same introductory scene shows that Iago dreads contempt as only a man can who habitually sneers at others. It also marks him as unscrupulous. The man who serves others only in order to line his own coat is a man after his own heart, a man with soul. And finally, this scene shows clearly that Iago is an egotist, and that he has the utmost pride in his own intellect.

> Were I the Moor, I would not be Iago.
> In following him I follow but myself ;
> Heaven is my judge, not I for love and duty,
> But seeming so, for my peculiar end :
> For when my outward action doth demonstrate
> The native act and figure of my heart
> In compliment extern, 'tis not long after
> But I will wear my heart upon my sleeve
> For daws to peck at.

How skilfully he can dissemble is shown in the following scene with Othello, where he protests his great indignation that anyone should have spoken ill of his commander.

Thus in the first scene we are introduced to Iago as he is : an egotist and a dissembler ; one who despises " love and duty," yet dreads contempt and hates the man who exposes him to it. It is in the closing soliloquy of Act I, however, that we get the most comprehensive single survey of Iago's character.

> I hate the Moor ;
> And it is thought abroad that 'twixt my sheets
> He has done my office : I know not if 't be true ;
> But I, for mere suspicion in that kind,
> Will do, as if for surety. He holds me well ;
> The better shall my purpose work on him.
> Cassio's a proper man : let me see now :
> To get his place, and to plume up my will
> In double knavery—How, how ?—Let's see :—
> After some time, to abuse Othello's ear
> That he is too familiar with his wife.
> He hath a person and a smooth dispose
> To be suspected ; framed to make women false.
> The Moor is of a free and open nature,
> That thinks men honest that but seem to be so ;
> And will as tenderly be led by the nose
> As asses are.

Here we have hatred of the Moor and desire for the lieutenancy iterated, as well as a new motive for hostility against Othello, viz. the suspicion that he has violated Iago's bed. The fact that Iago does not dwell upon that suspicion and work himself into a jealous rage over it has been taken to bolster up the " motive hunting " charge. But that Iago did suspect Othello is proved by Emilia's words later on (IV, ii) when, in speaking of the scurvy fellow that must have lied to Othello to make him suspicious of Desdemona, she says to Iago :

> Some such squire he was
> That turn'd your wit the seamy side without,
> And made you to suspect me with the Moor.

That Iago does not become jealous, but resolves upon punishment, reveals the very essence of his nature. He is cold and passionless, but vulgar and suspicious. He regards virtue and all women with contempt. That he considers the Moor of a free and open nature is no sign that he would not suspect him of unchastity, for he believes that all men are governed by their passions, as is shown by his method of handling them. Although absolutely unmoral himself, he prides himself on his ability to control the passions by which others are enslaved. This is one of the reasons for his high self-esteem. This self-esteem, however, is the cause of his most deep-set enmity for Othello. Of course, the " mere suspicion " that the Moor had been intimate with Emilia was as good a cause of action as though he really had been ; for the only place Iago could be wounded was in his pride, and the mere thought that there was a scandal to the effect that he had been cuckolded was wormwood to his pride. That Othello should refuse him the office of lieutenant had the same effect. Iago probably wanted the office for the honour and emoluments ; but he resented losing it because it reflected on his ability.

Those lines in the soliloquy just quoted in which Iago brags, as it were, of being a knave, may be a concession to Machiavellism—the type-villain— and the description to that extent is not strong characterization. The real Iago does not consider himself a knave, but regards his villainy as the worthy accomplishment of a well-organized brain. He would not call his villainy by its proper name, because he does not distinguish between right and wrong upon a moral basis. He judges men and deeds primarily from the intellectual standpoint instead of the emotional. The love of power of one sort or another is deeply bedded in man's nature, and Iago feels it. Coupled with his love of power is a consciousness of intellectual ability which he thinks should enable him to attain his desire. As a Machiavellian he believes that a man of intellect and strong will, unhampered by moral scruples, can and should triumph over the merely good. In fact, he regards goodness, i.e. altruism and self-sacrifice, as a sign of stupidity; and stupidity to him is the only wrong. Cunning, if successful, is right; success justifies all means. It is a source of great irritation to him, therefore, to see men who are simply, as he thinks, good, getting on in the world, while he with ten times their brains remains stationary and unrecognized. On general principle, then, Iago would feel antagonistic toward Othello. For Othello is good, and, in Iago's opinion, an ass easily led by the nose. Yet this man is his commander and a hero before the world. This in itself would vex Iago. But when Cassio, another stupid-good man, is placed over him by Othello, Iago reaches the limit of endurance. He resolves to " plume up his will," in other words, to vindicate himself as a Machiavellian, and to succeed by guileful wickedness.

Many a man sitting on the scorner's bench would like to wind men around his finger, but lacks the courage and the incentive to drive him to the possible wickedness by which it would have to be done. But Iago has the courage, and the repeated galling of his sense of superiority drives him on. He engages in hostilities with Othello more for the purpose of showing his own talents than for any other reason, but the other reasons are what make the display of his skill seem necessary. If he had been appointed lieutenant, the recognition might have pacified him ; but now he feels bound to test his own powers and to demonstrate that his intellect is superior to that of all the fools who are placed over him. Contemptuous of moral scruples, he engages in evil as affording the greatest scope to his talents. His active mind quickly conceives the knavery that will enable him to punish Othello, and at the same time be rewarded by Othello with the office he seeks, thus gratifying his ambition, satisfying his revenge, and flattering his self-esteem at once. Iago's ultimate defeat and downfall is tragic because the means in which he places his faith prove false. Egotism as a principle of successful action is proved to be unsound. He has failed in his own eyes : he has been stupid.

We have found that most Machiavellians appear unreal, and have indicated several reasons why Iago does not. Another reason is that he has just the shade of a conscience. It is not altogether the atrocities and stupendous crimes committed by these villains that render them untragic ; it is not only their tiger-like cruelty, nor yet the presence of malice without an impelling motive ; but also the total absence of any of the restraining motives common to mankind. Calculating villainy is not unnatural—it is hardly uncommon—but the execu-

tion of such villainy without a qualm, without remorse, without even a thought that it is wrong—
in other words, without giving any indication of
the elements of conscience—is so foreign to universal
experience as to strip such a villain, when represented on the stage, of the force of verisimilitude.
But when Machiavellian reasoning is seen to be
conjoined with a heart that feels, though it ignores,
the universal promptings of conscience, the villain
so endowed assumes tragic proportions. Some
such murmurings of conscience may be heard in
Iago's remark that Cassio

> hath a daily beauty in his life
> That makes me ugly.

Professor Bradley's query concerning this passage is
pertinent :[1] " Does he mean that he is ugly to
others ? Then he is not an absolute egoist. Does
he mean that he is ugly to himself ? Then he makes
an open confession of moral sense." In either case
he is not the hopeless embodiment of evil that has
been claimed. And this is just what our study of
other villains would lead us to believe. If Iago
delighted in evil simply for itself, he would create
the same impression of monstrosity that Aaron
does, and would not stir up so much discussion
among critics. If we regard those soliloquies in
which he ponders over the justification of his proposed villainy as the workings of a moral sense
within him, instead of as examples of " motive
hunting " (as this phrase is usually understood),
we shall come to a closer understanding of Iago's
character, and one that makes him more human.

[1] Supra, p. 234.

It is a matter of everyday experience that when a man wants to do something very much, but feels at the same time that he *ought not* to do it, he will create excuses for his conduct without ever waiting to have it criticized. But we do not say that his conduct is motiveless simply because he searches for reasons that will pacify his conscience.

Now something of this sort takes place in Iago. He craves power and seeks revenge. At the same time he professes contempt for the restraints of morality. Yet when he sets about the execution of his brilliant but immoral undertaking he is conscious that his design is evil and will be so construed, and in spite of his belief in himself, he cares something for the opinion of others. The lines about Cassio's daily beauty would prove that, as would the first scene, wherein he betrays a dread of contempt. Consequently he tries to convince himself that his action is right. He knows perfectly well that if Othello has abused his bed he would be justified in making an attack upon him; consequently he brings that motive up. We have seen that this was a perfectly sound motive in that the suspicion grated on Iago's sense of superiority, the gratification of which is his leading motive. In this instance, however, he tries to present the action as a man might who was concerned in the right and wrong of the matter, and this I take for evidence of a moral sense within him. True, it is not made a great deal of, because the desire to assert his own intellectual superiority is too absorbing; but still it is there. This trace of conscience is the final touch given by Shakespeare to render his character more lifelike.

How Iago is to carry out his wicked undertaking is not apparent at first ; but desire stimulates ingenuity, and he soon has the main features of his plot outlined in mind. The first step in the plot is to involve Cassio in a broil that will cause him to lose his position. This Iago accomplishes by getting Cassio drunk and setting Roderigo on to pick a quarrel with him. The first step is successful, but Iago is not yet appointed lieutenant, and Cassio may be reinstated. Nor is the desire to set Othello on the rack yet satisfied. With devilish acuteness he sees the means for accomplishing all his aims at once. Knowing that Cassio may win his office back by the intercession of Desdemona, Iago urges him to petition her, but takes care to render his efforts useless by making this very intercession the means to inflame Othello's jealousy. Chance plays into his hands, and he succeeds in all his schemes. At the end of the third scene of Act III, Othello, after suffering torments, exclaims :

> Now art thou my lieutenant.

Things have gone further than Iago anticipated, however, although no further, perhaps, than suits him. Othello demands proof of Desdemona's guilt and the death of Cassio. The danger and the necessity for meeting it, stimulate Iago to even greater activity. He is perfectly willing that Cassio should die, for Cassio may upset his plot at any time. Besides, he suspects him too with his nightcap. With amazing audacity Iago lies about the handkerchief and engages Cassio in a conversation that proves to Othello his guilt, but which might have been interrupted and the whole plot exposed at any moment by Othello's rushing in and attempting to slay Cassio himself, or demanding an explanation.

Two events now contribute to the catastrophe and lead up to the final event which Iago did not foresee. Othello's rage far surpasses anything Iago had anticipated, and leads to the murder of Desdemona. Though Iago had not foreseen that Othello's jealousy would demand such extreme measures to satisfy itself, he quickly adapts himself to circumstances, and himself suggests the means of death. The other event is the failure to kill Cassio. Roderigo is successfully despatched so that his dangerous knowledge can do no harm, but Cassio is merely wounded and lives to testify against Iago.

The cause that finally overthrows Iago, however, is the confession of his own wife, who, when she hears of the deceit practised upon Othello, exposes the villainy of her husband. Iago had never dreamed that his wife's unselfish love of Desdemona could rise above her fear of him, and in such ignorance of noble human motives lay his tragic error.

Iago's intellectual ability is the very salt of his character. It is not only the plot which holds us fascinated, but the source from which the plot springs—Iago's brain. Iago is an artist. As Hazlitt says : " He is an amateur of tragedy in real life, and, instead of employing his invention on imaginary characters or long-forgotten incidents, he takes the bolder and more dangerous

course of getting up his plot at home, casts the
principal parts among his nearest friends and connections, and rehearses it in downright earnest,
with steady nerves and unabated resolution."[1]
Naturally enough, therefore, Iago steals our admiration, for he appears to be the poet.   Other
admirable traits in him are his perfect poise, his
fearlessness, the quickness and courage with which
he sees and acts upon an opportunity, the readi-
ness with which he reads the minds of others.   If we
could detach these characteristics from the purpose
to which Iago directs them, they would appear in
themselves forms of goodness.   Without them Iago
would be not only unworthy but unbearable.   But,
of course, without them, Othello would not have
been imposed upon and there would have been no
tragedy.

Iago's intellect, however, is not of such a remarkable calibre as to make us suspend judgment upon
his wicked deeds.   Owing to the fact that the play
has two protagonists, one good, the other a villain,
it is impossible to say with certainty what the
effect would be if Iago were the only hero in the
play.   Would the audience feel deep tragic emotion ?
It seems doubtful.   Judging from the tragedies
already analysed, we should experience—in a successful villain-hero play—a feeling of mystery and
awe at the waste of great talents.   Richard III was
great enough to arouse these sensations, but the
same can hardly be said of Iago.   The tragedy of
Othello does, indeed, produce a most profound
effect, but the emotions of pity and sadness which

[1] *Characters of Shakespeare's Plays*, London, 1817, p. 54.

the tragedy arouses—pity for unmerited suffering, sadness for the irretrievable loss of noble qualities —are due to the fate of Othello, not of Iago. Though Iago terrifies us, he arouses no pity. In *Richard III* all of the emotions which we felt were occasioned by the villain himself. In Iago's disposition there is something mean which is inseparably connected with his admirable traits and which prevents them from affecting us as powerfully as do the admirable qualities in Richard's more aspiring nature. Richard is swayed by passion ; Iago is cool and calculating. Richard's passion is lofty ambition ; Iago is moved by hatred and revenge, which are base. Iago aims to humiliate those who are good, in order to justify his egotism ; Richard crushes others only in order to raise himself. He murders the innocent if they block his upward passage, but regal power, not their humiliation, is his object. Richard never stoops to torment his victims. Iago does ; he takes pleasure in the suffering of Othello. Moreover, Richard is the more versatile of the two villains. He possesses fully as much courage as Iago, and is besides a great warrior and statesman. He also manifests a greater cunning ; he outwits politicians who have been trained in the same school of suspicion and deceit as himself. Iago, though exhibiting remarkable skill in the given situation, confines his operations to two men—Roderigo, who is stupid, and Othello, who is too unsuspecting by nature to be quick in detecting, or skilled in analysing base actions.

Iago's intellect, as a matter of fact, is of a very limited range. Within a small circle of circum-

stances he is very acute; he knows all about
selfish instincts in men, and can turn them to his
use; and when he practises upon a man who has
never analysed other people's motives he is remarkably successful.   But it is not every good man who
would have been so easily led as Othello.   Fancy
how quickly Hamlet, who toyed with Rosencrantz
and Guildenstern, would have seen through Iago.
Iago knows nothing about goodness as a great
intellect does, and he suffers defeat on that account.
He is terrible, because, though not wholly evil, he
is lacking to such an extraordinary extent in the
feelings which bind humanity together, and because
he is so successful in applying his disintegrating
principles in the given situation.   But the meanness
in his disposition will not absent itself from our
thoughts, and its presence prevents such good
traits as he possesses from stimulating tragic
emotions to the degree that they otherwise might
if joined with villainy less base.   And finally, his
talents are not of a magnitude to make us feel that
the world has suffered a profound loss in ridding
itself of the villain who possesses them.   How
tragic, we may exclaim, that such a man as Othello
should be at the mercy of Iago!   But we would
never exclaim: How tragic that Iago's noble
strength should be so misemployed!   How tragic
that the world should lose such genius!

IX

MIXED REVENGE TYPE

MARSTON'S two plays, *Antonio and Mellida* and *Antonio's Revenge*, were published in 1602. They were entered on the Stationers' Register in 1601, but, according to Schelling [1] and Wallace,[2] were acted as early as 1599 by the Paul's boys. If such is the case, these plays were written before *Othello*, but Shakespeare's play is not the sequent of Marston's productions. Piero, the villain in *Antonio's Revenge*, has certain traits in common with the Aaron-Eleazar type, but he is not related to this type as a link in that chain of development which culminates in Iago. Moreover, the play of *Othello* does not belong to the revenge-for-a-father type of tragedy of which *Antonio's Revenge* is a direct descendent, containing motives of both the *Old Hamlet* and *The Spanish Tragedy*. In it are to be found the revenge for a father, vacillation on the part of the avenger, the appearance of the ghost of the murdered man urging the son to revenge, madness, intrigue and counter-intrigue to increase the stage business, and a final scene of horror resulting in the murderer's death.

In an earlier chapter a distinction was drawn

[1] I, 555.   [2] *The Children of the Chapel*, p. 70.

between kinds of revenge. It was shown that
revenge arising from hatred and offended pride was
unjustifiable, and that an avenger moved by such
motives was always a villain. Lorenzo was such a
villain, and Barabas was the same type pushed
forward as hero. Aaron and Eleazar belonged to
this type, but were differentiated by Senecan cruelty,
and by universal motiveless malignity. Iago represented the type perfected and humanized. On the
other hand, we found that revenge for a father or
son was justified as a code, and that such avengers
as Hamlet and Hieronimo, who acted from a sense of
duty, were never villains. They are, however,
usually the heroes of the plays in which they appear.

Now in *Antonio's Revenge* both types of avenger
appear. Antonio seeks revenge for the death of his
father, whom the villain, Piero, because of jealous
hatred, has murdered. Piero bears a close resemblance to Lorenzo, but takes a far more important
part in the action than Kyd's villain. In fact to a
reader not saturated with the traditions of revenge
tragedy, he would appear to be the protagonist,
although repellent. Andrugio, Duke of Genoa, and
Piero, Duke of Venice, have been mortal enemies;
but at the end of the first play they celebrate an
apparent reconciliation by a marriage contract
between Antonio, son of Andrugio, and Mellida,
daughter of Piero. In *Antonio's Revenge* Piero
poisons Andrugio; murders Feliche (Antonio's
friend), on the pretence of having found him in
Mellida's embraces; strangles his own accomplice,
Strotzo; plots to murder Antonio and marry Maria
(Antonio's mother); but he is finally outwitted and

killed by Antonio and Feliche's father, who survive
the action.

It must be admitted that Piero's rôle is at least
as important and prominent as Antonio's.   He so
monopolizes the action during the first two acts that
we are led by his soliloquies, his numerous plots,
and his horrid crimes to believe that his revenge,
lust, and ambition are to constitute the plot.   But
after the appearance of the ghost in Act III, revealing Piero's villainy and exhorting to revenge,
Antonio shares the honours as hero.   Nevertheless,
Piero continues to plot and to take an aggressive
part until the end.   As late as the trial scene in the
fourth act his accomplice accuses Antonio of having
contrived Feliche's murder.   Having no further use
for the accomplice, Piero thereupon strangles him.
The news of Antonio's death, which Antonio has
given out to save himself from arrest, is also reported
in this scene, and the shock of the news kills Mellida.
These events keep the villain in the foreground and
give an impression of success to his actions ; for the
death of Mellida is indirectly his fault, and it removes one more virtuous character, besides increasing the suffering of Antonio.   Moreover, of the two
leading characters Piero alone suffers death at the
end of the play, while Antonio lives on, which circumstance strengthens the impression that the
action represents Piero's tragedy.   The tragedy
really has two protagonists, just as *Othello* has.   In
the latter, however, though Iago directs the action,
Othello is so strongly characterized, his part is so
sympathetic, his career so tragic, that we never
forget his importance, but are more inclined to

regard him as the only protagonist.   In *Antonio's Revenge*, on the other hand, the revenge motive of the injured son is quite subordinated to the melo-dramatic devices originally introduced to accelerate the action.   As Piero brings about, or takes part in, so many of the striking scenes, the impression made by him is the one we are likely to carry away with us from the play.

The primary motive for Piero's acts is revenge, but revenge as entirely inexcusable as Lorenzo's. He takes us into his confidence in the very first scene, and tells us why he hates Andrugio.   He pro-fesses to have loved Maria, and to burn with rage against his rival for winning her affections.   But his love is selfish, sensual, and base.   Not for a moment does he forget himself and act blindly from passion, but pursues his rival and his rival's son deliberately and cautiously with an eye to his own advantage at every turn.   Indeed the motives of love and revenge will not explain all of his actions. Coupled with these motives is political ambition. After Andrugio's death he intends to kill Antonio, for his death will free Mellida for a future advan-tageous match, and enable Piero to gain the duke-dom of Genoa by marrying Antonio's mother.

> *Pier.*   Antonio lives : umph : how long ?
> ha, ha ! how long ?
> Antonio pack'd hence, I'll his mother wed,
> Then clear my daughter of supposèd lust,
> Wed her to Florence heir.   O excellent !
> Venice, Genoa, Florence at my beck,
> At Piero's nod.   (II, i, Bullen's ed.)

The means he takes to accomplish his ends are notably Machiavellian.   He poisons Andrugio ; he employs an accomplice, Strotzo, to murder Feliche ; and then treacherously strangles Strotzo.

> Why thus should statesmen do,
> That cleave through knots of craggy policies,
> Use men like wedges, one strike out another,
> Till by degrees the tough and knurly trunk
> Be riv'd in sunder. (IV, i.[1])

Piero believes and acts on Gentillet's maxim (III, 23), which says : " A Prince ought to have a turning and winding wit, with art and practise made fit to bee cruell & unfaithfull, that he may shew himselfe such an one when there is need."

> *Pier.* I'll seem to wind yon fool with kindest arm.
> (II, i, 56.)

Note also his soliloquy after he has had his conference with Strotzo, who is to accuse himself of having been Antonio's tool :

> So, so ; run headlong to confusion :
> Thou slight-brain'd mischief, thou art made as dirt,
> To plaster up the bracks of my defects.
> I'll wring what may be squeezed from out his use,
> And good night Strotzo. (II, ii, 2, 18.)

When conspiring Antonio's death Piero first defames him by having Strotzo accuse Antonio of having murdered his own father. Machiavelli discusses such "policy" in *The Prince* (VII), and Gentillet mentions it in one of his maxims (III, 2).

---

[1] Cf. *The Spanish Tragedy* in the lines following Lorenzo's order for the execution of his accomplice, Pedringano :

> Why so, this fits our former policy,
> And thus experience bids the wise to deal.
> I lay the plot : he prosecutes the point ;
> I set the trap : he breaks the worthless twigs,
> And sees not that wherewith the bird was lim'd.
> (III, iv, 39, *Temple Dra.*)

So far Piero might be said to be acting as a true
disciple of Machiavelli.   But he likewise partakes
of all the melodramatic traits that the appearance
of previous villain-heroes had caused to be associated
with Machiavellism.   When he exclaims :

> I am great in blood,
> Unequalled in revenge. . . .   (I, i, 19)
> I have been nursed in blood, and still have suck'd
> The steam of reeking gore ;   (II, i, 20)

we are carried back to the ghoulish boasts of Barabas
and Aaron.   In a manner comparable only to that
of Aaron, Eleazar, and Seneca's villains, he gloats
over his wickedness ;   revenge when successful gives
him almost a physical satisfaction.

> Swell plump, bold heart ;
> For now thy tide of vengeance rolleth in. (II, ii, 219.)

> He grieves ; laugh, Strotzo, laugh. He weeps.
> Hath he tears ?   O pleasure ! hath he tears ?
> Now do I scourge Andrugio with steel whips
> Of knotty vengeance.   Strotzo, cause me straight
> Some plaining ditty to augment despair.
> Triumph, Piero : hark, he groans, O rare !
>   (II, ii, 135.)

Malicious as Piero is, however, exulting as he does
in the torture of his victims, his malignity does not
embrace all mankind as in the case of Aaron and
Eleazar.   Nor is it entirely motiveless.   His breast
is swollen with vile lust and venomous hatred,
elements which though loathsome are at least in his
case understandable.   Sexual lust is a new motive
in a Machiavellian villain, and occurs again in only
one or two later plays.   It is, however, the most
striking element in Piero's character.   Although he

intends to marry Maria, his passion will bear no
nobler name than that of lust, and this beastly
appetite repeatedly oppresses us with its prominence.

> *Pier.* Maria, love, Maria ! she took this aisle.
> Left you her here ? On lights, away !
> I think we shall not warm our beds to-day.
>
> (III, i, 130.)
>
> Sit close unto my breast, heart of my love :
>
> .   .   .   .   .
>
> Thy husband's dead : life of my joys most bless'd,
> In that sapless log, that press'd thy bed
> With an unpleasing weight, being lifted hence,
> Even I, Piero, live to warm his place.
>
> .   .   .   .
>
> . . . Dost love me, fairest ? Say.
>
> .   .   .
>
> Why, then, Io to Hymen, mount a lofty note,
> Fill red-cheek'd Bacchus, let Lyæus float
> In burnish'd goblets ! Force the plump-lipp'd god.
> Skip light lavoltas in your full-sapp'd veins !
> 'Tis well, brim full. Even I have glut of blood :
> Let quaff carouse. (V, ii, 24.)

It is hardly necessary to state that *Antonio's
Revenge* is not a successful villain-hero tragedy.
The emotions which Piero inspires are unworthy of
tragedy. His crimes in themselves are offensive,
and his lustfulness makes him more repulsive than
all his crimes. Moreover, Piero has nothing great
about him to offset his villainy. He is neither intellectual, courageous, nor versatile ; but base, murderous, and malicious. He has not a single redeeming
feature in his character. It is impossible to sympathize with the motives of such a man, or to experience any tragic emotion at his death. Even terror
is wanting. Whatever fear he arouses is confined to
the first two acts ; after the appearance of the ghost

there can be no doubt as to his ultimate fate. And finally, the character of Piero is so lacking in verisimilitude, his language is so unreal, the play itself so sensational, that sober credence in what is happening before us is not for a moment possible.

It is a pity that Marston was unable to fulfil the promise given in the Prologue of tragic treatment. Instead, however, of giving us a true picture " of what men were and are," or of focussing his powers upon the delineation of a heart " pierced through with anguish," he produced a melodrama full of exciting situations. The introduction of the ghost to reveal Piero's crimes is but one of the many melodramatic touches that prevent us from taking the tragedy seriously. There is a startling climax or harrowing scene in almost every act. In the second scene of Act I, when Antonio and his mother are joyfully united, the one expecting the appearance of his love at the window, the other hoping to join her husband, the curtain is drawn before Mellida's window and Feliche's body, stabbed full of wounds, appears. Following hard on this shocking reversal comes Strotzo with the news of Andrugio's death. Maria swoons, and Feliche's father closes the scene with a fit of madness. In the second scene of Act II we are startled by the groans of Mellida coming from the prison grate ; in the same scene Antonio learns of Piero's passion for his mother, and is immediately confronted by them both. In the first scene of Act III Andrugio's ghost rises at midnight to reveal Piero's villainy ; the ghosts of both Andrugio and Feliche unite in crying Murder ! Murder ! and Antonio stabs Piero's son. In the following scene when Maria draws the curtains of her bed she is confronted by her husband's ghost. In the first scene of Act IV Antonio appears disguised as a court fool at the trial scene where Strotzo is strangled and Antonio accused of patricide. At this accusation Mellida faints, and shortly afterwards is reported dead. Then follows a scene in which Pandulfo and Antonio appear all but mad with grief, and finally swear revenge over Feliche's grave. The next and final act contains the banqueting scene, the masque, and the torturing of Piero. There is never a quiet moment in the play.

The appeal of melodrama is instantaneous, because it is so exciting; but it is temporary. Tragedy, on the other hand, vindicates itself slowly, but its appeal is more lasting, because it treats of the interrelation of real character and situation, and thereby offers a profound criticism of life. As Marston's plays were very popular he was soon imitated, especially by Tourneur and Webster, who never allowed the stage business to drag after they had learned Marston's useful trick.

Chettle's *Hoffmann*,[1] which is usually classed with the revenge-for-a-father type of play, came out about 1602, when this type was being revived. It has little in common, however, with the earlier plays in which the hero sought revenge for a murdered father. The original motive is the same, but the treatment of the motive is entirely different. Instead of following in the footsteps of Hieronimo or Hamlet, Hoffmann becomes a Machiavellian, and uses fraud, treachery,

[1] *Hoffmann*, by Henry Chettle, reprinted with emendations by H. B. Leonard, 1851; ed. by R. Ackermann, 1894.

poison, and murder to attain his ends. Revenge as
a justifiable code has disappeared ; hesitation based
on doubt or moral scruples has vanished ; Antonio
has merged into Piero ; the avenger has become the
villain. It was stated above that in the Kyd type
of revenge play the avenger was always the hero
but never the villain unless the dramatist failed to
justify the code of revenge. *Hoffmann* is one of
these exceptional plays. Chettle takes an avenger
for his hero, but fails to justify his deeds.

Hoffmann's father having been put to death on
false suspicion by the Duke of Luningberge by
means of an iron crown heated red hot and fastened
to his temples, the son resolves upon revenge.
There is no ghost to cry *Vindicta !* but the skeleton
of Hoffmann's father rattling in the wind, as it
hangs suspended from a tree where Hoffmann has
placed it, serves to remind him of his wrongs. The
avenger's first victim is Otho, the young son of
Luningberge, who is washed ashore with his servant
Lorrique from a wreck before the cave where
Hoffmann dwells. The burly avenger manifests no
Hamlet-like hesitation, but at once kills Otho by
means of the red-hot crown. He then strips the
flesh from the bones of the corpse and hangs the
skeleton beside that of his father on the tree. How
far this tragedy diverges from the revenge type
originated by Kyd is at once apparent. By this one
act, too revolting in itself to permit of sympathy or
even justification, the avenger's real task is done.
The rest of the play consists of the kind of intrigue
that the earlier dramatists assigned to the Machiavellian villain in order, probably, to fill in the action

before the revenge. Assuming the disguise of his victim, and accompanied by Lorrique, whom he uses as an accomplice, Hoffmann proceeds to the court of Otho's uncle, Ferdinand, who, having never seen his nephew, adopts the disguised villain into his own family. Thus firmly established, Hoffmann proceeds by means of trickery, poison, and murder to get rid of a round half-dozen of Luningberge's innocent relatives. He is about to exterminate the whole family when he is overcome for the moment by lust for Otho's mother. He is then betrayed by his accomplice, whom he mistrusts but stabs too late, and is finally caught in a trap set by his enemies, and executed by means of the same fatal crown that had caused the death of his father and of Otho. He dies cursing.

The whole play is a tissue of improbabilities dependent for interest upon intrigue and violence. The hero himself is at no stage of the action a sympathetic figure. Possessed by the demon of revenge, he determines in soliloquy to make the deeds of Atreus and Medea look pale, and he comes near doing it. After his first harrowing crime, which is the result of deep-seated hatred and revenge, he goes about his murders with that light-hearted Machiavellian spirit which delights in demonstrating the efficacy of wickedness. Ambition and, later, lust usurp the place of revenge as a motive for his actions. But this change is unnatural. He does not belong to that class of heroes whose genius for power makes their very wickedness attractive. Egotism, lordly pride, and a belief in his ability and right to dominate others do not set off his character and lift his crimes out of the mire of the common-place as they do in the case of Richard, or even of Barabas. In fact, when we first see Hoffmann, he appears excessively morbid, and reminds us of one who has been crushed—though unwilling to admit it—by superior strength, and who therefore broods over his wrongs. Then the transition from morbid brooding to Machiavellian ambition, accompanied by jovial cruelty, takes place without a convincing psychological explanation. In short, Hoffmann is a type of the monstrous, not a human being. Consequently his existence on the stage does not terrify us ; but the bloody scenes shock us. It might be expected that we should experience some satisfaction from the villain's death, but it in itself is too cruel to leave us at the close of the drama with any feelings that could be called elevated, "purged," or even satisfied.

X

CHANGING TYPE
THE MALCONTENT AND TOOL VILLAIN
AS REVENGER

In no play is the influence which Marston exerted
by increasing the stage business and developing the
intrigue more marked than in Cyril Tourneur's
Revenger's Tragedy, which was entered on the
Stationers' Register in 1607. In its atmosphere of
blood, lust, and morbid passions it carries us back
to Seneca. But the play is not moulded in Senecan
form, nor does it possess any of the technical marks
of classical tragedy. As the title indicates, it is
primarily a tragedy of revenge ; but the majority
of the motives that mark the main plot of the Kyd
type of revenge play have disappeared and only the
motives of the sub-plot remain. The hero seeks
revenge not for a father but for a poisoned sweetheart. The ghost has disappeared, though the hero
treasures the skull of the deceased lady as Hoffmann
did the skeleton of his father. Revenge is no longer
a solemn duty justified as a code and approved by
the audience, but springs from a malicious desire
for retaliation. Vendici, the hero, never vacillates
from doubt ; neither grief nor heavy responsibility
drives him mad ; he delays, but delays in order to

engage in activities which have nothing to do with
his revenge. *Hoffmann* is what we might call a
mixed type of play, for the avenger seeks revenge
for the death of a father, but is nevertheless a villain.
The author seems to have been anxious to stage a
play of the revenge-for-a-father type because that
type was popular at the time, but to have been unwilling to omit any of the Machiavellian traits that
had held the attention of theatre-goers during the
fifteen years immediately preceding the production
of his own play. But he crowds all the characteristics into the nature of one person, thereby creating
a villain who is untrue to life. The *Revenger's
Tragedy*, on the other hand, represents a changing
type. There is no intention on the part of the author
to portray either an avenger of the Hamlet type, or
a Machiavellian villain. Instead of either, we have
an unsuccessful, discontented, cynical philosopher—
a malcontent ; a man neither good nor great, but
vindictive and energetic enough to avenge by underhand means a specific injury. The passions portrayed are low, which is not the case in either of the
above-mentioned types.

The tragedy is laid in an Italian court of the most
corrupt manners, where vice is made the rule not the
exception of human nature. Vendici, the malcontent, has been brooding for a long time over his
wrongs ; and, when the play opens, he is waiting
an opportunity to murder the lascivious old Duke
who has poisoned his betrothed. There is no good
reason why he should not stab the Duke at once,
except the necessity for a melodramatic plot ; for
no external objects are put in his way, and neither

conscience nor doubt as to the identity of the guilty
person deters him. He grumbles at the wickedness
and injustice of the world, and harps upon the revenge which he is about to take, but makes no steps
towards remedying his condition. He manages by
disguising himself to get intothe service of the Duke's
eldest son, Lussurioso, a gentleman of the same
stamp as the father. In this position he is employed as tool villain to seduce his own sister. He
acts the part of pander from a morbid curiosity to
test the virtue of his mother and sister. The interest
of the play is heightened by this repetition of the
villainy of the father in that of the son, Lussurioso,
and the temptation scenes are in themselves effective,
but these scenes are diversions from the main plot.
After Vendici has satisfied his curiosity he drops the
part of pander, and finally despatches the old Duke
by a most gruesome trick. He then turns upon the
son, whom he pursues for the remaining two acts
and at last kills in a masque.

But this is by no means all that is presented on
the stage. Vendici's rôle of tool villain is but one
of the many means adopted for stirring melodramatic
excitement in the absence of a serious plot to hold
the attention by the conflict between character and
circumstance. The Duchess' youngest son is tried
for rape ; Spurio, bastard son of the Duke, commits
adultery with his step-mother ; Lussurioso, thinking
to kill Spurio, wounds his own father, and is on that
account sentenced to prison ; Ambitioso and Supervacuo, sons of the Duchess, endeavouring to get
their younger brother out of prison by a trick, send
him to the scaffold by mistake, and free Lussurioso,

whom they hate ; Ambitioso, Supervacuo, and Spurio, as maskers, dance into the room where Lussurioso is holding revels after becoming Duke, intending to kill him, but finding him already dead, fall upon each other ; those who are with them are apprehended, but Vendici unexpectedly confesses the murder of both Lussurioso and the old Duke, and is sentenced to die.

As melodrama, in realism of effects and mastery of horror, as a study in morbid psychology, the *Revenger's Tragedy* remains unsurpassed. But the plot has not the ring of truth ; it is made to order and unconvincing. The separate scenes hold the attention, but are not carefully connected. Events do not follow in a natural sequence of cause and effect. After the second catastrophe, which consists in the murder of Lussurioso, it is simply a *coup de théâtre* to have Vendici confess his crimes to Antonio and so bring upon himself the death sentence.

The hero himself takes no hold on our sympathies. He is, as we have indicated, far removed from the old types of avengers ; at the same time the characteristics with which Tourneur has endowed him do not relieve the blackness of his villainy nor lift him into the sphere of the heroic. The Hamlet type of avenger held our sympathy because he was good ; his vengeance was void of malice. The Machiavellian villain compelled our admiration by his audacity even when we could not pardon his crimes. But Vendici is neither a Hamlet paralysed by grief, nor a Barabas consumed by fiery energy. By failing to justify Vendici's crimes in the eyes of the spectators,

Tourneur rendered his hero a villain ; by failing to
blend great strength and ability with the wickedness
in his character, he left his villain with no qualities
that fascinate.

The wide gap that separates Vendici the malcontent from the revenge-for-a-father type of hero is,
however, no broader than the chasm which opens
between him and the Machiavellian villain. Vendici
is a cynical critic of life rather than an active per-
former. He is a malcontent, with only one impelling
motive—revenge ; not an egotist driving over others
with haughty disdain. He uses poison, but that
alone does not constitute a Machiavellian. Of the
other characteristic traits Vendici shows none. He
does not startle us by his boldness—he is barely
courageous. He is not an ambitious man, not a
political intriguer. Nor, on the other hand, is his
revenge like that of Barabas, Iago, or Piero, an
instance of wicked guile triumphing over innocence.
If he uses craft it is only against those who are more
wicked and vile than himself. The punishment and
pain which he actually inflicts do not extend beyond
those who have done him an injury, although in his
triumph over them he is thoroughly malicious.
Even his ill will toward the world is not the malignity of an Eleazar, but the grudge of a malcontent,
of a man professing some morality, hating men's
vices but not men themselves. He never exhibits
that satisfaction which may be called intellectual,
and which is so peculiar to the Machiavellian, in
seeing a systematic course of evil prevail over moral
principles. In fact, Vendici recognizes the sanction
of moral law, but does not always distinguish

between right and wrong in a given situation. He
regards the conduct of the Duke and Lassurioso as
wicked and vile, and hates them for it, but he does
not consider his own murder of them wrong. The
reason that he is a malcontent and cynic is because
he sees that wickedness and baseness, which he
considers beneath him, flourish in social circles far
above him. But when he suffers a personal loss
because of the prevalence of that same wickedness,
he does not consider his own actions in murdering
and torturing the wicked ones wrong. Murder to
get rid of a person whose life is a source of incon-
venience is criminal ; retaliation which involves
murder is justifiable. For the Duke to poison his
betrothed was wrong ; to avenge her death by
poisoning the Duke is right. But this is a confusion
of moral values which does not deceive the audience.
It is the spirit of the Corsican vendetta. Vendici's
revenge springs from a natural desire to retaliate,
for it is natural for a man to wish to slay the murderer of a person so near and dear to him as his
affianced wife. Nevertheless, retaliation in this
particular case is abhorrent. The reason that
Vendici's revenge does not appear justifiable to the
audience is not that Tourneur purposely wrought
for such an effect, but that the hero's cause for vengeance has grown cold with fifteen years' waiting ;
that he is not bowed down by sorrow ; that no
religious motive, symbolized in earlier tragedies by
the ghost, urges him on ; that he is not moved by
love or duty, but altogether by hatred ; and, finally,
his revenge is unjustifiable because it is so very
malicious.

Vendici's malice, though limited to those who have injured him, is of the most venomous kind. He smears poison on the mouth of the skull of his murdered sweetheart and kills the Duke by forcing him to kiss the poisoned mouth. Before allowing him to die, however, he compels him to witness the lascivious embraces of the Duchess and his bastard son. He seeks to render the last moments of Lassurioso mentally as well as physically agonizing by whispering in his ear that it is he, Vendici, his supposed tool, who has murdered him as well as his father. Now, the mind of a man who could conceive such torture is repulsively morbid ; his actions insufferably base. Stabbing a man is noble compared with such odious villainy. The fate of such a creature could never stir the depths of tragic emotion. The playwright has depicted varying shades of depravity, instead of portraying the tragic conflict of an individual trying to shape his own ends. His hero exhibits no elevation of character, his plot is not a unit, the events are not inevitable, the situations are representations of the particular rather than the universal in human nature ; consequently, though he has succeeded in producing a stirring melodrama, he has not succeeded in producing a first-rate tragedy.

The character of the revenger had degenerated so completely by the time Webster came to write his *Duchess of Malfi* [1] that he made no attempt to justify revenge as a code but portrayed the revengers Ferdinand and the Cardinal as unsympathetic villains and criminals, treating their crimes realisti-

[1] *John Webster*, by E. E. Stoll, published Mudge & Son, Boston, 1905.

cally and relegating them to their natural place in
the moral scale.   Tourneur's hero-villain, Vendici,
is too unreal a character and too much contaminated
by sin to arouse any sympathy ; but, as we have
seen, it is not owing to Tourneur's recognition of
moral values that this is so ; he does not endeavour
to reveal the absurdity of such a convention as
revenge ; on the contrary, he tries to elicit some
sympathy for his hero by suggesting piety—incon-
gruous enough—and less loathsome guilt in a world
where all is vicious, base, and lustful.   The moral
censures which he puts into Vendici's mouth seem
conceived to elevate his character and to cleanse it
of the pollution which clings to the members of the
court where the tragedy is laid.   Moreover, Vendici's
final speech, after he has been condemned to death,
would indicate that he considered his life well spent
in losing it to satisfy his revenge.[1]   Webster, on the
other hand, paints vice as vice, and crime as crime.
Though much depravity exists, his world is still
moral ; wickedness meets with the judgment it
could receive only in a world where moral law
existed.   Webster's vision is limited, however ; his
world is small and shut in, and the result is seen in

---

[1] *Ven.*   May not we set as well as the duke's son ?
Thou hast no conscience, are we not revenged ?
Is there one enemy left alive amongst those ?
'Tis time to die when we're ourselves our foes :

.   .   .

And if we list, we could have nobles clipped
And go for less than beggars ; but we hate
To bleed so cowardly : we have enough,
I'faith, we're well, our mother turned, our sister true,
We die after a nest of dukes.   Adieu !

This is not the language of ridicule ; rather, it upholds the code
of revenge.

the emotional effect of his tragedies, but within this small world he sees things clearly and relates them to each other with no confusion of right and wrong. Tourneur, with a vision equally limited, an outlook equally cynical, saw everything with a nearsighted eye—blurred, confused, indistinct ; and the result in his plays is moral confusion. Of the whole brood of villains in the *Revenger's Tragedy* only one of them, so totally depraved is the world represented, recognizes that there is anything reprehensible in seduction and adultery, or even in murder and poisoning. The one who rails against evil is the hero, but even he sees nothing but virtue in his own villainy. Consequently there is no tragic force in the deaths that take place on the stage. For, although the villains die by poisoning and violence, every one dies that way in Tourneur's world ; and in dying the villains do not feel that retribution has overtaken them, but simply misfortune. The truth is not driven home that the fate of the guilty is any more inevitable than that of the guiltless. This is where confusion lies, this is why no tragic effect is produced.

In the *Duchess of Malfi*, though he does not reach the highest peaks of tragedy, Webster yet emerges from the realm of melodrama. In his tragic world men of power and position are tyrannical, cruel, crafty, and faithless, but there are other beings who are tender and loving, noble and self-sacrificing. Good has its effect as well as evil ; the innocent may suffer from the heartlessness and ambition of the wicked, but they can die heroically and keep alive the good in others, while sure retribution awaits the violator of moral law. Even those who oppressed by circumstances have become callous from crime, have sparks of goodness in them which, when fanned to life, light them to heroic things. Above all, Webster humanizes his chief characters. The good are not misrepresented as bloodthirsty, and the wicked are not made to boast of their crimes, call themselves villains, defy God, and act generally like the proverbial stage villain ; they are much more self-contained. As a rule the characters who suffer bring upon themselves their punishment ; but this is not always so—it is not the case with the Duchess herself—and consequently Webster comes perilously near to rousing in us simply painful feelings without calming them in the end. If some attempt were not made to reconcile us by the deaths of Ferdinand and the Cardinal, and by the return of Bosola to goodness, we could hardly call the emotion we experience in any degree pleasurable.

From the standpoint of dramatic technic the *Duchess of Malfi* is not properly the tragedy of the Duchess at all, but of her brothers, Ferdinand and the Cardinal, and of Bosola. The fate of the Duchess is profoundly pathetic, and, owing to the dramatic art lavished upon her portraiture in order to make her end pathetic, she stands out more prominently than any other figure during the first four acts ; but she is absolutely without tragic guilt, and the play continues for another act after her death to bring about the tragic doom of the three villains who have sought to advance themselves by her destruction. It has been urged [1] that the Duchess pulled her fate upon her own head by her rashness,

[1] Stoll (supra), p. 130, and note 3.

but such an interpretation of the play does not
correspond to our emotional experience. If her so-
called rashness is tragic guilt, then she deserves to
suffer somewhat, if not to such an extent as she does.
But this is not the case. The Duchess is a widow,
a woman of independent fortune and position,
legally not under the control of her brothers at all.
These brothers, in order that they may inherit her
estate, forbid her to marry ; but they have absolutely
no right to do so, and she is not bound by any law,
human or divine, to obey them ; her right to marry
is indisputable. That she was murdered for marrying in despite of her brothers' threats is evidence of
monstrous evil in the world, but not of tragic guilt
in her action. There might have been rashness in
her conduct if she had married openly, for then she
and her husband would have risked instant death.
It would have been the rashness of daring to do
anything however blameless in defiance of a criminal's
orders. But so far is her actual conduct removed
from rashness that she manages to conceal her
marriage for many years and to rear three children.

The fate of her brothers, however, follows from
their treatment of her ; her murder is their tragic
guilt. They employ a villain to torture and kill
her, and in the end both are killed by the villain
whom they had employed. They are not, however,
villain-heroes ; they are simply villains. Though
they conceive the wickedness that leads to their
sister's death, they hire a tool to execute it. They
themselves are not set forth in high relief ; they
are not thoughtfully psychologized ; their conflict
with moral law does not interest us, but only the

effects of their machinations upon the Duchess. The art which might have been used to centre our attention upon them is expended upon Bosola, the tool whom they employ. It is his activity which constitutes the action of the play. The Duchess wins our attention and sympathy by her suffering ; Bosola takes an equal share of our attention because it is he who torments her. After her death our interest centres upon him exclusively. The author takes pains to make him an interesting character. And, finally, Bosola's death is in itself tragic. He therefore becomes the villain-hero.

Now, Bosola is not a Machiavellian, not an egotist, not an advocate of wickedness, but a poor Italian gentleman whom circumstances force to crime against his will. It seems almost impossible to modern minds that such wickedness as Webster describes could ever really have existed ; it seems still more unlikely that men of culture could have stooped to Bosola's crimes ; and yet, if the historians of the Italian Renaissance may be believed, such atrocities were little more than commonplace. So deep were the passions, so corrupt was that little world, that men of high standing might droop and languish until they had accomplished some murderous revenge. Courtiers might be assassins ; and reputable scholars, driven by loss of occupation, might sell themselves to princely criminals.[1] As we have seen, other dramatists were not unfamiliar with the depravity of court life, but, with the

---

[1] Benvenuto Cellini : Autobiography ; J. A. Symonds, *Shakespeare's Predecessors*, p. 35 and p. 393 ; " The Italian Renaissance in Italy—Age of the Despots," Chapter VIII.

exception of Tourneur, they had all chosen to represent it through the Machiavellian villain. Taking advantage of the villain figure to which audiences had become accustomed, Webster ignored the Machiavellian type and substituted in its stead as a type for special study the poor Italian gentleman [1] whose motive was that a man " must live," wishing, apparently, to show in Bosola how deeply tainted such a man could become and still possess remnants of virtue.

The various characteristics that form Bosola's nature had been utilized, indeed, by other writers to tag their villains and heroes, but had not been used in such a way as to make these men lifelike. Marston introduced the figure of the malcontent in his play called *The Malcontent;* Tourneur made Vendici a malcontent and caused him to simulate the part of tool villain, though he was not such indeed. But Bosola unites in good earnest the parts of malcontent, tool villain, and revenger. With such intensity does Webster draw the character of Bosola that the three apparently contradictory rôles which he plays lose their incongruity and unite to form a character appealing to the imagination as unique and realistic. To be sure, it is not very difficult to conceive of a tool villain as a malcontent, especially if he has been forced into his trade by want, and if his previous mental training has been of such a kind as to enable him to see the ignominy of his position. But Webster has gone further. Recognizing that every criminal has his human side, he has endowed such a man with a certain underlying

[1] Bosola is his own creation ; not in his source.

fund, or residuum of goodness, and with courage
enough to revolt and become a resolute avenger.

In the process, however, of raising the typical
tool villain from his subordinate position of mere
tool to the central position of protagonist where he
excites sympathy, pity, and even admiration, a
great change has taken place in the character of the
villain, as may be seen by comparing Bosola with
Flamineo of *The White Devil*. Flamineo, like
Bosola, makes it plain that he serves to live, but
unlike Bosola he shows little aversion to the service
exacted of him. He curses his mother for bringing
him into the world without any provision for his
welfare, but he curses her also for interrupting his
efforts to advance himself by playing the pander
between his own sister and Brachiano. He is flippant
and coarse and base, and remains base until his
death. The causes which have contributed to make
him a tool are not presented in such a light as to
awaken sympathy, but the depravity which he
displays while serving as a tool excites our aversion.
He is a thorough villain, yet, as he but serves another,
he is not the villain-hero.

Bosola from the beginning reveals a higher nature
in his conversation. He is educated, and is something of a philosopher. In the midst of all the corruption of the Italian court he is the only one of the
wicked characters who shows a sign of goodness.
His bluntness and keen analysis of the evil about
him make him a sympathetic figure. He does not
stoop to flatter, and does not love wickedness, yet,
surrounded by so much evil, with no particular
moral standard to support him, but only an inclina-

tion and sympathy for goodness, he sinks, tempted by need, into the mire around him. Poverty and social conditions drive him to crime ; crime sears his conscience ; and he becomes the wicked tool of a monstrous tyrant. The sympathy engendered by him in the first act, however, is so considerable that when he turns spy and becomes the executioner of the Duchess we are stunned rather than alienated. It hardly seems possible that the Bosola we have known could have done this. But that the horror of his crime, the resignation and goodness of his victim, should have their effect upon him and re-awaken all his good instincts seems perfectly natural. This time his good instincts conquer. He resolves to take upon himself the punishment of his employers who, without a drop of humanity, have planned and commanded the tortures which have shaken even his hardened soul. It is his tragedy that when once reformed he should kill the one man he is trying to save, and be killed himself by the villains whom he now seeks to punish. It is true that remorse alone does not transform him into an avenger ; the in-gratitude of Ferdinand, who treats him with con-tempt and leaves him as penniless after his frightful service as he was before, is necessary to sting him to action. But his independence having once asserted itself, all his natural emotions come rolling in and carry him forward on their crest as the agent of divine vengeance.

Bosola's resolution to tear himself from his evil moorings in order to serve at last the cause of justice restimulates our exhausted emotions, and points to reconciliation. In the act which elapses after the death of the Duchess, Bosola displays resolution, bravery, sympathy, and willingness for self-sacrifice. In short, he becomes the avenging hero. His part is so important that he shares an equal place with the Duchess in our memories. And if a play so harrowing and so full of horror can also be said to please, it is not simply because Ferdinand and the Cardinal suffer as they deserve, but because, by the development of Bosola, goodness and bravery are shown to exist even in a soul as spotted as that of a tool villain. The insufferable strain produced by the painfully pathetic death of an innocent woman is somewhat relieved, and our confidence in human nature restored by the fortitude with which Bosola pursues his end and meets his death.

But when all is said, the *Duchess of Malfi* still shows many flaws. It is not a tragedy of the first order, for it does not produce the same emotional effect as such tragedies as *Hamlet, Othello, King Lear,* or *Macbeth* for instance. Nothing could exceed in pathos the death of the Duchess, but in this scene the tragedy reaches its high-water mark. Pity is present, but without the fear that accompanies tragic guilt, and the result is simply painful. We are conscious of no such pleasure as we derive from a Shakespearean tragedy, for that which is simply painful has no cathartic effect. The Duchess by the very force of this scene remains the chief figure, but her death, though dignified, reveals no law of human destiny connecting man's sufferings with his previous actions. Such a connection between character and circumstances is attempted with the villains, but as they are not the really sympathetic figures, the highest tragic effect is lost. The unity of plot is broken ; there is the tragedy of the Duchess on one side, and that of her murderers on the other. If her fate is intended for the centre of interest the play should close with her death, though that would be very painful in the absence of tragic guilt ; if the fate of villainy is intended for the main issue there should not be so much time and effort expended on the villains' victim, for it puts the villains in a subordinate position. After the fourth act the centre of interest is shifted ; the fifth act might not unreasonably be called " Bosola's Revenge." Such a change mars the unity of the play.

Considering the tragedy as it stands, however, we find that in addition to the flaw in plot construction it is weakened by the nature of the character-drawing, and above all by the choice of action itself. For Ferdinand and the Cardinal we have not even the sympathy of understanding, so shadowy are their characters. Many a reader who pities from his heart the fate of the Duchess, fails to understand why her brothers forbade her to marry—what their motive could have been. Bosola, on the other hand, is well enough understood, but understanding him convinces us that he is not such stuff as tragic heroes are made of. The dramatist makes a real effort to portray a tragic struggle in his breast by showing his unwillingness to play such a part as tool villain, but the effect is not transporting. When Ferdinand bribes him, he replies :

> *Bos.* Take your devils,
> Which hell calls angels : these cursed gifts would make
> You a corrupter, me an impudent traitor :
> And should I take these, they'd take me to hell.

Ferd. Sir, I'll take nothing from you that I have
    given :
There is a place that I procured for you
This morning, the provisorship o' the horse ;
Have you heard on't ?
  Bos. No.
  Ferd. 'Tis yours : is't not worth thanks ?
  Bos. I would have you curse yourself now, that
    your bounty
(Which makes men truly noble) e'er should make me
A villain. O, that to avoid ingratitude
For the good deed you have done me, I must do
All the ill man can invent ! Thus the devil
Candies all sins o'er ; and what Heaven terms vile
That names he complimental.

The struggle presented is that of a needy gentleman
hesitating between a sort of loyalty to the man who
has saved him from want, and obedience to his
better instincts. Bosola's unfortunate condition,
however, is not over-emphasized, to say the least,
and his yielding is very abrupt ; a good deal is left
to the imagination.

But this is not the chief fault, for Bosola does win
our sympathy. The weakness of the tragic effect as
far as it concerns Bosola is due to the fact that his
struggle with moral law is not of sufficient magnitude ; Bosola is not great enough for the struggle
to be profound ; he has goodness in him but no
grandeur of soul. Those same influences mentioned
by Nietzsche [1]—viz. the influence of the greatness
or smallness of the aims, of the intellectuality of the
means, and of the opposing forces and their value—
which led us to admire Barabas, lead us in this
instance to form an opinion of Bosola which is not
consistent with tragic dignity. The first impression

[1] See supra, p. 52, Chapter V.

which we received of Barabas, as well as of Richard,
was one of power. When by oppression in the one
case and ambition in the other these men are driven
to villainy, their daring, courage, intellectual ability,
and unscrupulousness bring on a struggle with
moral law which is terrifying in its intensity and
scope.[1] Now, Bosola is not a man of extraordinary
talents. He has been able neither to build up his
fortunes, nor to fortify his soul against the bitterness of poverty. He struggles against the cramping
circumstances of his life, but until the time of his
revolt his life has been a gloomy rather than a tragic
failure. He desires nothing higher than a comfort-
able income and social recognition, but is unable to
attain even these without selling himself. What is
there in such a man to awaken profound admiration ?
What is there in his struggle to shake us with terror ?
The struggle is interesting, excites sympathy, but
hardly rises to tragic dignity because of the squalid
motives underlying the man's conduct. We see
only the unwilling villainy of a tool who carries out
the malicious plots of others because his resource-
fulness is not great enough to put him by honest
means beyond the reach of want, and his moral
character is not strong enough to endure the hard-
ships of poverty. When he revolts, nobler motives
than formerly govern him. We applaud his revenge
because it is comparatively unselfish, and because it
requires courage. But his previous conduct has
been too wicked for us to lament his fall as that of a
morally good man, and yet the success of his former

[1] See the chapters in which these plays are treated for details
on which this statement is based.

villainy has not been due to qualities that are admirable from the æsthetic standpoint. Neither in his villainy nor in his revenge does he display the passion and will of a Barabas, the intrepidity and brilliance of a Richard, or the ingenuity of an Iago. As his soul has nothing particularly elevated in it, we condemn his villainy without, on the other hand, being able to admire to any great extent the source from which his actions flow, as we did in the case of the three characters just mentioned.

The most tragic effect possible is obtained from such a hero and from such an action ; but both Bosola and the situation in which he finds himself are rather exceptional. Even when idealized a tool villain is not a character possessing typical and universal value. We feel sure that Bosola and his wicked employers could never have existed anywhere but in Italy during the age of the despots. The conflict between good and evil is not brought home to us as in the case of *Othello*. The faults of the tragedy are the result of Webster's limited and cynical view of the world. He attempts to depict characters and a situation as universal which human experience refuses to accept as anything but exceptional. Consequently, though we sympathize with Bosola, admire some things about him, and even pity him, we are not carried out of ourselves and thrilled with awe. We do not look upon this tragedy as an exemplification of the ever-present and all-pervading mysterious laws of the universe.

XI

LATER AMBITIOUS VILLAINS

CYRIL TOURNEUR'S *Atheist's Tragedy* (printed 1611)[1] is a curious combination of several types of plays. It belongs in setting to the old type of revenge for a father, but the motives are very much modified. There is a ghost who reveals the murder, but strangely enough counsels the son to leave revenge to God ; there is not only hesitation on the revenger's part, but, with the exception of a moment of hot temper, a complete resignation of all activity to await the judgment of Heaven ; insanity manifests itself, but only in the actions of the villain ; melodramatic devices—graveyard scenes, presentiments, omens, etc.—are plentifully used, and a comic underplot keeps the stage in a bustle. The most significant change, however, is in the part played by the villain, who carries on the entire intrigue in the main action. The villain is, in fact, the hero, and this changes the nature of the play. The title is not at all misleading ; it is the atheist's tragedy. Both by means of soliloquy and of action D'Amville is made the protagonist. But though

---

[1] Thorndike (*Hamlet and Contemporary Revenge Plays*, published M. L. A., p. 135) and Fleay think this play was written before 1603 ; but Stoll, in the Appendix to his *Webster*, argues for a date approximately that of the printing.

the tragedy is a villain-hero play, the author does not attempt to exemplify the miseries of man's life where law and order are unable to protect the innocent from the wickedness of power, nor yet to fascinate by the marvellous talents of the villain. On the contrary, he has attempted to show that wickedness, no matter how carefully safeguarded by the devices of human reason, will come to light and be punished ; that natural law—i.e. the law of the survival and predominance of the fittest physically and mentally—is subordinate to a divine will, and therefore not dependable unless man's purpose in utilizing it is a moral one. In other words, God's providence is omnipotent. This moral is pointed directly at D'Amville, the atheist, and the revenge of a son for a father is subordinated to the working out of this moral. Even the sub-plot, which is entirely foreign to any motive of earthly revenge, has some bearing when connected with God's vengeance on atheism and immorality, for in it one of D'Amville's sons is killed, and all of the characters destroyed are vicious.

But the machinations of the villain and the disasters that follow upon his attempt at criminal self-assertion are confined within the limits of his own family connections. No far-reaching disorders, no convulsions of nature result from his villainy. There is no attempt to take the tragedy out of the home. The families concerned in the action are titled but commonplace. It is not the tragedy of a man of high estate, but a domestic tragedy, although the lack of intense realism and the presence of excessive romanticism disguise the type. We have, then, a domestic tragedy, with the setting of a revenge play, in which the dramatist, by making an atheist the protagonist, attempts to reveal the conflict between natural laws and God's will, and to demonstrate the ultimate triumph of the latter.

In treating the villain's character from a psychological standpoint the author of this play, which was written before the *Duchess of Malfi*, anticipates Webster. But D'Amville, whose character is the only one carefully studied, is ambitious, not revengeful. This presents the curious anomaly of a revenge play with an ambitious hero. But, although ambitious, D'Amville does not strive for political power ; nor does he entertain such visions of gold and jewels and world-wide influence as Barabas. In fact, his ambition is not of that extraordinary nature that fills us with astonishment and admiration. What he desires is to confer distinction upon the family name, in the neighbourhood where he lives, by acquiring an independent fortune for himself and heirs.

> *D'Am.* But let me call my projects to account
> For what effect and end have I engaged
> Myself in all this blood ? To leave a state
> To the succession of my proper blood.
> (IV, ii, Mermaid ed.)

In the effort to realize his desires, D'Amville shows certain Machiavellian characteristics. He scoffs at goodness and providence. In order to secure the wealth which he considers the only thing worth having he does not hesitate to murder his brother Montferrers, and to dispossess Charlemont, Montferrers' son, by means of trickery and the aid

of an accomplice. In order that he may have heirs
to inherit the property which he has acquired at
such a risk to his life and reputation, he marries
his eldest son, Roussard, to the wealthy heiress,
Castabella, who is betrothed to Charlemont. As
the son proves impotent, he himself attempts to
ravish her, and is only prevented by the unexpected
appearance of Charlemont. He thereupon trumps
up a charge of murder against Charlemont for
killing an assassin whom D'Amville himself had
set on.

Up to this point D'Amville is something of a
Machiavellian. He murders by means of accomplices ; he is hypocritical and treacherous as well as
atheistical ; and he laughs gleefully at the success
of his superior cunning. But he does not engage in
political intrigue ; he is not antagonistic to the world
at large ; he does not desire to get rid of anyone
but the Montferrers in order to inherit their property;
he takes no pleasure in the suffering even of his
enemies ; he does not kill his accomplice ; and he
does not use poison. In fact, his programme is
hardly large enough for a Machiavellian. Moreover,
after the point in the plot last referred to, his fortunes and his character undergo a marked change.
He had believed that nature was on the side of the
strong arm ; that if he succeeded by force or guile
in advancing himself, he need fear no such supernatural counterforce as retribution ; that what he
acquired rightfully or wrongfully by the natural
superiority of his own wit would not be taken away
from him by the unnatural intervention of Heaven.
He had believed that it was natural for his son to

have issue ; he had disbelieved that if he could circumvent mortal enemies any divine power would punish him for sacrificing the happiness of a young woman to his desire for heirs, even though he realized his ambition by the crime of incest. But now he is ironically mocked by the very nature in which he had placed his trust ; or, rather, by a power behind nature in which he had placed no trust at all. By the sudden death of his younger son one hope for the succession of his house is cut off. Hard upon this staggering blow to his pride comes the news that his elder son has died childless. With his faith in atheism rudely shattered, and half maddened by remorse, he attends the trial of his nephew. There he witnesses such stoicism and peace of mind on the part of Charlemont and Casta-bella when they face death together that he feels that he is in the presence of a power which he never understood. Incensed at this fortitude which he does not possess, demented by the failure of his cherished plans, he seizes an axe to kill his nephew, but knocks out his own brains instead. Staggering from the platform, convinced that God controls the laws of nature and that his fate is God's judg-ment, he confesses his crimes and dies.

Although finely conceived, D'Amville's character is not sustained, and in the end becomes grotesque. In the early scenes he arouses our interest and apprehension, for he appears to have the will, the strength, and the intellectual ability to carry out his evil designs. His failure is partly due to the inability of a wicked man to estimate the heroic moral qualities of the virtuous, and in so far is reasonable. It is partly due, also, to the providential death of his two sons. Although Sebastian is a reckless rake and Roussard a weak and sickly man, and both therefore likely to die before the expiration of the natural period of man's life, yet their deaths coming so suddenly and together, with the dramatist's moral purpose showing plainly behind the event, appear to be due to a most fortunate chance. Nevertheless, chance has its place in tragedy, and when employed, as here, ironically, is effective. But when we have said this we have exhausted the artistic merits of the tragedy. The plot as a whole is disconnected and highly improbable ; the ghost scenes are ridiculous ; and the multiplication of the elements of chance passes the bounds of credibility. By chance Montferrers makes his will in favour of D'Amville the moment he hears of Charlemont's death ; by chance the night is dark and stormy when he sets out for home ; by chance the servants, who are all drunk, put out the torches on this dark night so that the murder can be executed securely ; by the mechanical intervention of the ghost, Charlemont hears of the murder ; by chance the villain's pistol misses fire ; by chance Snuffe drops a sheet which Charlemont uses to disguise himself as a ghost ; by chance Charlemont is on the right spot to prevent D'Amville from injuring Castabella ; and finally, by chance, D'Amville kills himself instead of his nephew. This catastrophe in itself is melodramatic and absurd ; when added to the other elements of chance it causes the frail structure of the drama to collapse and to appear a jumbled heap of disconnected parts.

Though D'Amville himself is a strong man, the situations in which he has to use his strength are unconvincing, and the crimes which he commits border upon vulgarity instead of startling us into awe by their magnitude. We feel neither pity nor fear for the hero. Through the whole play runs the thread of the author's purpose to shake D'Amville's atheism by the enforcement of poetic justice. This moral purpose is so evident that it is unæsthetic. In the presence of a vulgar hero and unconvincing situations, with a didactic purpose confronting us, a tragic mood is an impossibility.

For ten years after the production of *Richard III* no effort was made to present in tragic form the story of the political ambition of a villain. Then came Jonson's *Sejanus*, which was acted in 1603. Sejanus shows many Machiavellian traits, but as Jonson refers constantly to classical sources for his interpretation of the character of his protagonist, it becomes next to impossible to say whether the portrait is simply the result of Jonson's classical studies, showing that he and Machiavelli were familiar with the same sources, or whether he was led to use his historical knowledge by his familiarity with the works of Machiavelli[1] and the numerous plays containing Machiavellian villains that had appeared by this time. At any rate the similarities in the characters of Sejanus and other Elizabethan villains are very pronounced.

In classing Sejanus as a Machiavellian villain of the ambitious type, one important distinction has to be noted. He is not himself a prince like Selimus,

[1] Cf. Meyer, pp. 89, 93, 100, 118.

Alaham, and Richard III, but a prince's counsellor. Moreover, and perhaps because of his subordinate position, he does not take the field of war, but confines his activities to the chamber.[1] He ministers to the desires and power of his ruler, but—and this is the real motive for his conduct—he also seeks to supplant him. He is, indeed, actuated by revenge in the case of Drusus, and this motive conforms his character even more closely to the mould left by the villains who had gone before him ; yet this motive is a minor one. As a matter of fact, in his divergence from the morbid revenger and from the bombastic slayer, and in his close attention to political business, he is the nearest approach to the real Machiavellian that we have had since Richard.

Although he is not a prince, Sejanus has a " turning and winding wit "[2] that almost enables him to circumvent Tiberius himself. He is cruel and faithless and altogether unscrupulous in the means he takes in seeking advancement. He " maintains factions and slays such as love the commonweale."[3] He is an atheist ; religion is to him a thing to be scoffed at or pressed into service as occasion dictates :

> 'Twas only fear first in the world made gods. (II, ii.)
>
> What excellent fools
> Religion makes of men ! . . .
>
> .   .   .   .   .
>
> I know not that one deity, but Fortune,
> To whom I would throw up in begging smoke
> One grain of incense ; or whose ear I'd buy
> With thus much oil.   (V, i.)

[1] Cf. W. D. Briggs, *Influence of Jonson's Tragedy*, Anglia, XXXV ; N. F. B., XXII, January, 1912.
[2] Cf. Gentillet, III, 23.
[3] *Ibid.*, III, 15.

The overturning of the goddess Fortune, when the omens prove unpropitious, illustrates his attitude towards rites and forms.

The political policy expressed in the following quotation, which is taken from the dialogue between Tiberius and Sejanus (II, ii), although it is in the manner of Seneca, is also quite in accord with the sentiments expressed in *The Prince* (XVII), the *Discourses* (III, 19 [377]), and certain maxims of Gentillet (III, 8, 9, 10, 13).

> *Sej.* Whom hatred frights,
> Let him not dream of sovereignty.
> *Tib.* Are rites
> Of faith, love, piety, to be trod down,
> Forgotten, and made vain ?
> *Sej.* All for a crown.
> The prince who shames a tyrant's name to bear,
> Shall never dare do anything but fear ;
> All the command of sceptres quite doth perish,
> If it begin religious thoughts to cherish :
> Whole empires fall swayed by those nice respects.[1]
> It is the licence of dark deeds protects
> Even states most hated, when no laws resist
> The sword, but that it acteth what it list.

He seeks to " altogether root out the blood and race of such as before governed,"[2] not as a prince but in order to become one. He even uses poison to work his will, although he does not rid himself of accomplices.

In addition to the relationship, based on the character of the protagonist, between this play and other villain-hero plays, the action of the play itself bears a certain resemblance to its predecessors. Sejanus begins his tragic career from ambition ; he

[1] *Ibid.*, II, 3.   [2] *Ibid.*, III, 4.

prosecutes it by means of intrigue ; a successful act
of revenge makes him over-bold ; and over-boldness
leads to his detection and sudden overthrow.

We have before us a villain-hero play with facts
and characters taken from history, and one written
by a man who did not allow the popular demand
for sensationalism to run away with him ; yet the
play is not a successful tragedy. In many of the
preceding plays we found that the presence of
sensationalism and the absence of verisimilitude
were enough in themselves to explain the failure of
such plays. On that account we were prevented
from determining just how much the villainy of
the hero had to do with such failure. In the present
instance also, technic is largely responsible for our
failure to respond emotionally to the tragedy.
The action is far too sluggish, and this sluggishness
is due to narration, to the failure to eliminate unnecessary details, and to spiritless characters.
But in this case another cause of failure is just as
apparent—the character of the hero himself.

The tragedy of *Sejanus* may, as Professor Schelling believes,[1] contain " one of the most consummate dramatic studies of historical character to be
found in the annals of literature " ; but when
read simply as a play, not as history, interest flags.
Dramatically, the minor characters are more interesting than Sejanus and Tiberius. Moreover,
the play contains too many narrations and orations
unnecessary to the plot. To allow Silius and
Sabinus to put us in touch with the situation by
their conversation is well enough ; but to allow

[1] *Elizabethan Drama*, II, p. 26.

them to run on page after page describing the merits of the dead Germanicus, who is only important because his children are in line, several times removed, to the throne, is tedious. To allow them to interpret the actions of Sejanus, instead of letting him speak for himself, may make a fine historic study of these individuals and their times, but throws Sejanus in the shade and retards the action, which is undramatic. In re-reading the play for the plot, after having become familiar with its general trend, one skips over these long descriptions as immaterial. The same might be said of the letters and orations of Tiberius. They are excellent as revelations of the historic character of the emperor. It might have pleased Tiberius to adopt such methods with the Senate, just as it might suit a lawyer in arguing a case to gather together all the points in favour of his client and to forestall all the arguments of his opponent, but such a process of presentation, weighty though it may be with a judge, is wasted upon an audience. The actor has to appeal to their emotions, not their reason. Realism, when it extends to tiresome details, is not always the most successful way of doing this.[1]

Another fault based upon too close an adherence to history is that the leading characters are lacking in passion. They may speak naturally, they may feel as Romans felt, but they are not swayed by passion, and passion is necessary to tragedy. Jonson did not " enlarge everything as a poet," as

[1] The object of Tiberius' enumeration of past events in the scene convicting Sejanus is undoubtedly to produce a dramatic effect by a surprising reversal, but the speech is so long that it defeats its object.

Marston in his preface to the *Tragedy of Sophonisba* suggested that he should have done, but tied himself down to relating events " as an historian." Occasionally he breaks away from this method, as in the trial scene of Silius (III, i), and the result is admirable. The fault to be found with this episode is that Silius is a minor character, but in this one passionate scene is allowed to call forth more admiration and emotion than the principal characters.

Still another feature of the play detracts from its dramatic interest. The situation presented is one where everyone puts up with tyranny, bears it, offers no resistance, suffers in silence. The Senate is servile. A few individuals resent the perversion of justice, but take no steps to oppose it. The good are stoics ; the mass is submissive. The villain acts, indeed, but we are not carried away by his actions before his fall, because he does not meet with antagonism enough. The struggle is not sufficiently keen. In fact, what is there for Sejanus to struggle with ? Not with his conscience, for he has none. Not with the good senators, for they realize their lack of power and bow to the inevitable. There is only one opportunity for a struggle, and that is with the emperor. Although Tiberius is represented as deceived by his favourite, he is not himself pictured as a particularly good man. Hence the struggle between him and Sejanus could not stir the fear that is aroused by a conflict between good and evil. To arouse any interest over their antagonism the dramatist must represent a clash of wits, an intellectual combat. And this is what is

attempted but not carried out. Tiberius having
become convinced of the guilt of Sejanus crushes
him without more ado. The hesitation and wavering, the doubt and final conviction that might have
been represented in action are all summed up in
the artful letter addressed to the Senate.

Such lack of poetic treatment is fatal to the drama
as a whole, irrespective of the villainous character of
the protagonist. Sejanus would not make a successful hero, however, even if the tragedy as a whole
were animated. And this for a particular reason : he
is not great enough. His Machiavellian character is
not complete : he is all fox and no lion. Sejanus
possesses that very meanness of spirit which clings
so tenaciously to our everyday conception of a
villain. Even the egotism which in the case of some
villains is so great as to stagger us and for ever
eliminate contempt, in his case almost degenerates
into conceit. He has none of Richard's greatness,
ability, or versatility ; nor is he built on the colossal
scale of Barabas. Consequently, his villainous
traits—his craft and treachery—having nothing
admirable to offset them, simply remove him from
our sympathies.

The most dramatic touch in the portrayal of
Sejanus is in the suddenness of his fall. If he were
great, or if the emperor against whom he aimed
were a particularly just man, the catastrophe
might arouse pity or suggest Nemesis ; but as it is,
in spite of the omens and the ironic worship of the
goddess Fortune, the fall of Sejanus leaves us cold.
The treatment of his body at the hands of the mob
is an incident intended, perhaps, to increase the

impression of the completeness of his fall, and to awaken a touch of pity, as for excessive punishment, but this incident is an appendage to the action proper, a detail shocking rather than pathetic, and quite unnecessary.

Much of what has been said of *Sejanus* is equally applicable to *Catiline* (1611). Both have the same faults of construction, and the figures of both are drawn from history. Seneca is again put under contribution, this time for scenes as well as dialogue.[1] From Seneca " Jonson borrowed the opening of *Catiline*, in which the Ghost of Sylla plays the same part as the Ghost of Tantalus in the *Thyestes ;* and when the oath of conspiracy is taken ' the day goes back,' and murmurings are heard from unseen speakers, ' as at Artreus' feast.' "[2] Like Sejanus, Catiline displays numerous Machiavellian characteristics but quotes no maxims. The use of maxims has a peculiar effect in branding a villain as a Machiavellian ; human beings do not talk so frankly about their own wickedness as do these blunt Machiavellians when they express their cynical and immoral sentiments in aphoristic form, but this touch of unreality, this affectation of the stage villain, is the very thing that associates itself with Machiavellism. Now Catiline does not impress us in such a manner, but analysis shows that all the traits of Machiavellism are to be found in his character. He is a political intriguer, with the nature of the lion and the fox. He has a very contemptuous opinion of men, yet knows how " to wind and turn men's minds that he may deceive

---

[1] Cf. Cunliffe, p. 94. [2] *Ibid.*

and circumvent them." [1]   He uses accomplices,
though he does not kill them.   He does not fear
" to be perjured, to deceive, and dissemble." [2]   He
is heartlessly cruel because he believes that it is
better to be feared than loved. [3]   He is an absolute
egotist. He is a man of " incests, murders, rapes " ; [4]
he is unscrupulous, ambitious, and vindictive.
He plots with Lentulus, Cethegus, Curius, and
others to secure for himself the consulship for
which Cicero is a candidate, and then to let loose
such destruction on all Rome as would make
Barabas turn in his grave with envy. To win
confederates to his treasonous plot he is artful and
perfidious ; to one he holds out command, to
another riches, to another the gratification of lust.
Others he stimulates by recalling their disgrace.
Especially is this true in the case of Lentulus, whom
Catiline promises to make king of Rome in accord-
ance with the decrees of an oracle.

The whole first act is truly admirable, for it
reveals the characters of all conspirators, and sets
Catiline in high relief. Neither his baseness nor
the vileness of some of his confederates is concealed,
and yet, because of the enormity of the crime which
he undertakes, the subtlety and penetrating insight manifested in its plan, and because of the
fearlessness with which Catiline attempts to consummate it, admiration as well as terror is awakened.
We await in suspense the issue of this conflict
between the wickedness of a subtle and powerful
villain, and the forces of law and order. Why, then,

[1] Gentillet, III, 19.
[2] *Ibid.*, III, 18.
[3] *Ibid.*, III, 9.
[4] Introduction.

do we rise at the close of the play somewhat tired as by a chapter in history, instead of thrilled with tragic emotion ?

Our disappointment is due solely to the undramatic construction of the play. By the end of the first act the plot is well under way, and the safety of Rome endangered. Cicero, however, is elected consul, and discovers the conspiracy. With the aid of Curius he gathers enough evidence to convince the Senate of the treasonous plot, and thereby brings about the banishment of Catiline. So far we have a complete action, with a beginning, middle, and end. But Jonson here makes the fatal mistake of substituting historical for dramatic truth. Aristotle's comments on the unity of action reveal the weakness of Jonson's tragedy. "Unity of plot does not, as some persons think, consist in the unity of the hero. For infinitely various are the incidents in one man's life which cannot be reduced to unity ; and so, too, there are many actions of one man out of which we cannot make one action. . . . The plot, being an imitation of an action, must imitate one action and that a whole, the structural union of the parts being such that, if any one of them is displaced or removed, the whole will be disjointed and disturbed. For a thing whose presence or absence makes no visible difference, is not an organic part of the whole."

Now the tragedy of *Catiline* as Jonson has constructed it may have several parts removed ; it consists of several actions. The first plot we have already outlined. It ends with the banishment of Catiline. Historically this was not the end of

Catiline nor of the conspiracy ; in order, therefore, to be true to history, Jonson added the other actions. The incident of the Allobroges may be removed without affecting the plot ; so may the death of the conspirators and the final battle with Catiline. By a different arrangement of the incidents—by dispensing with Cicero's endless rhetoric, or by delaying the introduction of his evidence until all the events that took place before the battle had been presented—in other words, by imaginative treatment, the play might have been made a unit with a single catastrophe. As it is, there is a triple catastrophe : the banishment of Catiline, his death, and the execution of the conspirators. We are worked up to each catastrophe and led to expect that it will end the play ; but the action goes on and on, and we have to adjust ourselves anew each time.

But there are still other defects which explain our lack of interest after the first two acts. Many of Cicero's orations — always long-winded and rhetorical, adapted to the Senate but not to the stage—are irrelevant. We are bored, instead of being held in suspense. Moreover, numerous comments made by other characters are also superfluous. What have the words of Cæsar and Crassus, and the suspicion attaching to them, to do with the action ? Nothing. They are merely thrown in because of their historic worth ; they lead nowhere : nothing is made of them. And finally, Catiline's downfall, though proceeding from his own inordinate ambition and crimes, has nothing inevitable about it. The fact that a conspiracy breeds agents against itself is not driven home. All is due to the excessive caution and laborious eloquence of Cicero—who is not the hero.

It is these faults of construction, and the abundance of rhetoric, not the fact that Catiline is a villain, that throws the tragedy out of the first class. For, in spite of the crimes he commits, and in spite of the wickedness attributed to him, Catiline is great enough, intellectual, energetic, and courageous enough to constitute a terrifying hero. In *Sejanus* both the character of the hero and technical defects reduce the effectiveness of the tragedy ; in *Catiline* the hero's character is no drawback, but technical faults are even more fatal than in *Sejanus*.

The Devil's Charter. Only two other tragedies of the villain-hero type remain to be considered, and both were acted in the years intervening between *Sejanus* and *Catiline*. The one, *Macbeth* (1606-10), is a total departure from Machiavellian models ; the other, *The Devil's Charter, A Tragedy containing the Life and Death of Pope Alexander the Sixth*, by Barnabe Barnes (1606), has for its chief figures Alexander VI and his son Cæsar Borgia, two men cited constantly as models by Machiavelli and referred to by Gentillet. This tragedy contains motives enough in blood, violence, and horror to supply a whole school of dramatists.

The leading motive, like that of *Faustus*, is supernatural—a compact between the Pope and the Devil—and the plot suffers from the usual difficulty confronting the dramatist who takes the infernal compact for his theme, viz. how to fill in the time between the signing of the contract and the arrival of the devil to claim his own. In the play before us the author proceeds on the chronicle plan of filling in the acts with melodramatic scenes dealing with the passion and intrigue that marked the ambitious careers of Alexander and Cæsar Borgia.

The speeches of the Pope and Cæsar, revealing their characters, are full of Machiavellism. Barnes undoubtedly had in mind Gentillet's maxims (III, 18, 21), advocating perfidy and deceit, when he made Alexander speak the following lines :

> *Alex.* You must not be so ceremonious
> Of oaths and honesty, princes of this world
> Are not prickt in the books of conscience,
> You may not break your promise for a world :
> Learne this one lesson, looke ye mark it well,
> It is not alwaies needful to keep promise,
> For princes (forc'd by meere necessity
> To passe their faithfull promises) againe
> Forc'd by the same necessity to breake promise.
>
> (I, 4.)

The policy of a " turning and winding wit " is well understood by Cæsar :

> *Cæ.* And for your more instructions learne
>   these rules !
> If any Cedar in your forest spread,
> And over-peere your branches with his top,
> Provide an axe to cut him at the roote,
> Suborne informers or by snares entrap
> That king of Flies within the Spider's Webbe :
> Or els ensnare him in the lion's toyles.
> What though the multitude applaud his fame :
> Because the vulgar have wide open eares
> Mutter amongst them and possesse their hearts
> That his designements wrought against the state
> By which yea wound him with a publick hate.

> So let him perish, yet seeme pitifull
> Cherish the weaknesse of his stock and race
> As if alone he meritted disgrace.
> Suffer your Court to mourne his funeralle,
> But burne a bone-fire for him in your chamber.
>
> (I, 4.)

The maxims on religion and dissembling, as well as Machiavelli's theory of war, are brought out in the Pope's reply :

> *Alex.*   Cæsar delivereth oracles of truth.
> 'Tis well said, Cæsar, yet attend a little,
> And binde them like rich bracelets on thine armes
> Or as a precious jewel at thine eare.
> Suppose two factious princes both thy friends
> Ambitious both, and both competitors,
> Advance in hostile arms against each other
> Joyne with the strongest to confound the weake
> But let your wars foundation touch his crowne,
> Your nearest Charity concernes your selfe ;
> Els let him perish ; yet seeme charitable.
> Lively dissemble faith and holinesse,
> With clemencie the milke of Majestie :
> As if you were meerly compos'd of vertue :
> Beleeve me Candy things are as they seeme,
> Not what they bee themselves ; all is opinion :
> And all this world is but opinion.   (I, 4.[1])

Cæsar goes further than his father in carrying out what by this time had become the typical Machiavellian policy of murdering accomplices. He hires Frescobaldi to help kill Candy, and then throws him along with Candy into the Tiber ; he hires Baglioni to shoot Rotsi, but arranges to have Baglioni drink of Rotsi's poisoned wine, so as to die himself shortly afterwards.

The action, which consists almost entirely of the deviltries of these two Machiavellian villains, is in-

[1] Cf. *The Prince*, XXI ; Gentillet, II, 1 ; III, 18, 20, 21, 22, 26, 27, 28.

artistic, not because of sensationalism, but owing
to lack of unity. Alexander is represented in the
prologue, and in the dumb show which follows, as
having become Pope through bribery and the
assistance of the Devil, granted in compliance with
the terms of a contract signed in blood. By its
stipulations Alexander understands that he is to
have free scope to do as he pleases for eighteen
years, at the expiration of which time the Devil may
claim his soul. The first four scenes of Act I are
expositional. The rest of the play is a fulfilment of
the programme announced in the prologue :

> Our subject is of blood and tragedie,
> Murther, foule Incest, and Hypocrasie.

The crimes of which Alexander is guilty are summed
up by Cæsar (who is guilty of almost as many) as
simony, bribery, extortion, usury, murder, incest,
and sodomy. The final scene, which has some power,
presents the Pope's death struggle. He is represented as being in the Devil's power : the contract
which he supposed covered eighteen years is shown
by another reading to be for eleven years and seven
days, and the hour of its expiration has now arrived.
After experiencing the pangs of remorse and the
fear of hell, Alexander is carried off by the devils.

A strong effort is made to produce an effect of
unity by this last scene, but without success. In
fact, the final scene is more effective when read by
itself than when taken in order ; its seriousness and
spiritual force are marred if we come to it in the
mood induced by the merry trick of the Devil in
the preceding scene. In that scene the Devil

descends to the level of the Vice in the Moralities by
stealing into the buttery and changing the position
of a bottle of poisoned wine so that the Pope and
Cæsar drink of it. Our emotions in recalling the
play, or even when reading it, are singularly untragic ; the absence of causal sequence between
actions is fatal. There is the wide gap between the
prologue and the final scene which almost causes
us to forget that Alexander has sold himself ; the
separate scenes, although they portray character,
do not represent that character developing ; and
finally the catastrophe on its realistic side does
not spring from any previous act of the Pope's.
He is not poisoned because he has poisoned others,
but because the Devil is a practical joker. Moreover, the necessity of his dying by poison at all is
entirely superfluous if his time to die has come by
the terms of the compact. It is suggested, indeed,
that the Devil has seen fit to end Alexander's life
on the appointed day by the same means which the
Pope has employed to advance his own worldly
prosperity, but there is a conflict here between the
supernatural motive and the rational which is
confusing. A sense of the inevitableness of the
catastrophe, so essential to tragedy, is wanting.

XII

MACBETH (1606–10)

THE story of *Macbeth* in naked outline is a tale of as
cruel and barbarous villainy as any we have hitherto
studied. A Scottish nobleman and general receives
under his own roof in treacherous hospitality his
aged monarch to whom he is bound not only by
blood and loyalty but by innumerable tokens of
love and high honours recently conferred, and slays
him with his own hands in order to usurp his throne,
and then, to secure his position, resorts to such
massacre of men, women, and children as drives
his subjects to rebellion and involves his country
in civil war.

But, it will be said, such an outline is misleading ;
it omits the most essential features of Macbeth's
character, and does not reveal him as he really is.
The objection is valid, and consequently makes it
necessary to prove that Macbeth is a villain according to the terms of our definition before we endeavour
to interpret the art that endows such a frightful
story with tragic dignity.

That Macbeth violates received standards of
morality for a selfish end is certain. The crown of
Scotland is the end ; treason and murder are the
means he adopts to gain it. That he knows what

he is doing and carefully deliberates upon the nature of the act and its possible results is only too evident from his soliloquies. Our first effort will be to establish this point, thus fixing Macbeth's responsibility. That the murders are committed " wilfully " would almost seem to follow if the other facts are true, but as the degree of wilfulness in a crime affects materially our sympathy for the criminal it will be further necessary to study Macbeth's character with that element in view. The other devices that contribute to the total tragic effect will then be considered.

Macbeth's start of surprise, as contrasted with Banquo's coolness, when the witches first hail him with his future titles, instantly produces in us the suspicion that he has been harbouring guilty thoughts before, and that the witches have, as it were, read his mind. There is nothing absolutely to prove that his mind had previously been filled with treasonous ambition, still, the suspicion lodges in our mind and explains the rapidity with which murderous thoughts crowd upon him as soon as Ross announces the fulfilment of the first of the prophecies.

> *Macb.* (*aside*).   Glamis, and thane of Cawdor !
> The greatest is behind.

This is not much to fasten an accusation on, but the dramatic tenseness produced by the words is due entirely to our belief that Macbeth is dallying with the temptation to gain that greatest which lies behind by wrongful means. We are sure of it a moment later.

> *Macb.* (*aside*).   Two truths are told,
> As happy prologues to the swelling act
> Of the imperial theme.—I thank you, gentlemen.

(Aside) This supernatural soliciting
Cannot be ill, cannot be good : if ill,
Why hath it given me earnest of success,
Commencing in a truth ?   I am thane of Cawdor :
If good, why do I yield to that suggestion
Whose horrid image doth unfix my hair
And make my seated heart knock at my ribs,
Against the use of nature ?   Present fears
Are less than horrible imaginings ;
My thought, whose murder yet is but fantastical,
Shakes so my single state of man that function
Is smother'd in surmise, and nothing is
But what is not.   (I, iii, 127–42.)

He is actually contemplating murder at this early
stage, before any opportunity has presented itself.
True, he closes his soliloquy by saying that he will
resign himself to chance, but the sequel shows that
he does no such thing.   The fact that he drops plotting temporarily because the thought of murder
quite upsets him, has its place in estimating his
character, in showing that he is not totally conscienceless, but such scruples do not, of course, relieve him
of responsibility, legally or morally, when later he
overcomes them and commits the crime.   When
Macbeth decided to leave all to chance he was in
direct line to succeed to the throne ; he had only
to await the old king's death.   But in Scene 4 this
is changed.   The king designates Malcolm his heir.
Chance has put a block in Macbeth's way and he at
once decides to trust to chance no longer.

Macb. (aside).   The Prince of Cumberland !
    That is a step
On which I must fall down, or else o'erleap,
For in my way it lies. Stars, hide your fires ;
Let not night see my black and deep desires :
The eye wink at the hand ; yet let that be,
Which the eye fears, when it is done, to see.

So far Macbeth has been thinking chiefly of the
end ; but Scene 7 reveals his knowledge of the
wickedness and possible consequences of the criminal
action, and shows his realization of his own freedom
to act or refrain, so clearly that his responsibility is
established beyond a doubt.

> *Macb.*   If it were done when 'tis done, then 'twere
>   well
> It were done quickly : if the assassination
> Could trammel up the consequence, and catch
> With his surcease success ; that but this blow
> Might be the be-all and the end-all here,
> But here, upon this bank and shoal of time,
> We'ld jump the life to come.   But in these cases
> We still have judgment here ; that we but teach
> Bloody instructions, which, being taught, return
> To plague the inventor : this even-handed justice
> Commends the ingredients of our poisoned chalice
> To our own lips.   He's here in double trust ;
> First, as I am his kinsman and his subject,
> Strong both against the deed ; then, as his host,
> Who should against his murderer shut the door,
> Not bear the knife himself.   Besides, this Duncan
> Hath borne his faculties so meek, hath been
> So clear in his great office, that his virtues
> Will plead like angels, trumpet-tongued, against
> The deep damnation of his taking-off ;
> And pity, like a naked new-born babe,
> Striding the blast, or heaven's cherubim, horsed
> Upon the sightless couriers of the air,
> Shall blow the horrid deed in every eye,
> That tears shall drown the wind.   I have no spur
> To prick the sides of my intent, but only
> Vaulting ambition, which o'erleaps itself
> And falls on the other.

In spite of all these reasons strong against the
deed, he commits the murder. Lady Macbeth's tongue
is a sufficient spur to prick the sides of his intent.
Her influence is to be admitted at its full force ; it

may even have been the determining factor in his actions. If we did not admit her influence, her existence, dramatically, would be superfluous. But the fact that she urges him to the crime, though it may lead him to commit it, does not excuse him. By instigating her husband to murder, Lady Macbeth becomes an accomplice and we have two criminals where before we had one.

Act II, Scene 1, presents Macbeth awaiting the signal for the crime. There is no longer any hesitation between doing and not doing, though his nerves are strained to the breaking point ; his vivid imagination portrays the horrible fitness of the hour for the deed, but does not deter him from it.

> Thou sure and firm-set earth,
> Hear not my steps, which way they walk, for fear
> Thy very stones prate of my whereabout,
> And take the present horror from the time,
> Which now suits with it. Whiles I threat, he lives :
> Words to the heat of deeds too cold breath gives.
> *(A bell rings.)*
> I go, and it is done ; the bell invites me.
> Hear it not, Duncan, for it is a knell
> That summons thee to heaven or to hell.   *(Exit.)*

This is sufficient evidence to establish Macbeth's responsibility for the murder of Duncan. He realized more perfectly than anyone else the heinousness of his offence, and yet committed the crime. For the atrocities that follow, the assassination of Banquo, the slaughter of Macduff's wife and children, Macbeth is so manifestly responsible as to leave no room for argument. The tragedy being primarily the representation of the disintegration of a character once started on the downward path, Macbeth shows no further signs of compunction. The task left for the critic, rather, is to show how the hero regains our sympathy, for by the end of Act IV, owing to Macbeth's superstitious terror and inhuman cruelty, it is totally lost.

It must be admitted, then, that Macbeth deliberately, and for a selfish end, violates standards of morality sanctioned by the audience. He is also wilful; but not so wilful as Richard, Barabas, Eleazar, or Hoffmann, who never hesitate a moment over their crimes, need no accomplice to spur them on, never show a sign of remorse, and, with the exception of Richard, never give evidence that they possess a conscience. Hence our lack of sympathy for their actions, and indifference to their fate. Although Macbeth is a villain according to our definition, that definition does not require that a villain be conscienceless, remorseless, and at peace with himself. We admit Macbeth wilful, but insist that his wilfulness is modified, among other ways, by conscience, and that this modification of wilfulness is one of the chief dramatic means by which our sympathies are enlisted.

We cannot agree with those critics who assert that Macbeth is conscienceless and never feels remorse, who say, " The apparition (of Banquo) is not, like the ghosts who throng the tent of Richard III, the offspring of a moral revolt. It is born of fevered blood, not of conscience, and though it turns Macbeth's cheek white with terror, it stirs in him no feeling of remorse." [1] " Of conscience, in the strict sense, neither (Macbeth nor Lady Mac-

---

[1] Boas, 419 : *Shakespeare and his Predecessors.*

beth) is possessed." [1] To say this, however, is to
be untrue to our imaginative experience. We do
not feel that Macbeth is utterly depraved during
the performance of the tragedy ; if we did we should
have no sympathy for him, as our analysis of other
tragedies goes to show. But since the evidence that
leads critics astray in thus estimating Macbeth's
character is to be found in the play itself, it is well
worth careful examination. The result of certain
analyses of this kind is to prove that Macbeth never
pictured the horrible aspect of his deed except to
get an idea of how it would look to others and so
enable him to estimate his own chances of executing
it without being detected or punished ; that every
poetic line of world-weariness merely indicates
regret for lack of success, not remorse for the deed.
Professor Moulton has devoted a chapter to this
method of proving Macbeth a shallow, conscienceless
villain, devoid of any real sense of right and wrong,
and sections of his article are here quoted as being
as typical and convincing as any on the subject.

" Macbeth's character is a type of commonplace
morality, the shallow unthinking and unfeeling
man's lifelong hesitation between God and Mammon.
[The lines uttered by Lady Macbeth beginning
' Thou wouldst be great '] assert distinctly that
Macbeth has no objection to the evil itself, but only
a fear of evil measures which must be associated to
a practical mind with failure and disgrace." To
support this statement Professor Moulton quotes
the passage beginning " Stars, hide your fires." He
then continues : " Macbeth has torn himself away

[1] *Ibid.*, 422.

from the banquet, and, his mind full of the desperate
danger of the treason he is meditating, he ponders
over the various motives that forbid its execution.
. . . Yet, if Macbeth's famous soliloquy be searched
through and through, not a single thought will be
found to suggest that he is regarding the deep considerations of sin and retribution in any other light
than that of immediate practical consequences. . . .
Macbeth is willing to take his chances of the next
world if only he can be guaranteed against penalties
in this life. (By the end of the twelfth line of the
soliloquy beginning ' If it were done when 'tis
done ') he has reached no higher consideration in
reference to treason and murder than the fear that
he may be suggesting to others to use against himself the weapon he is intending for Duncan. Then
his thoughts turn to the motives against crime,
which belong to the softer side of our nature.[1] At
all events it is clear that this is no case of a man
blinded for the moment to the emotions which
resist crime ; and as we hear him passing in review
kinship, loyalty, hospitality, pity, we listen for the
burst of remorse with which he will hurl from him
the treachery he has been fostering. But, on the contrary, his thoughts are still practical, and the climax
to which this survey of motives is to lead up is no
more than the effect they will have on others : pity

> Shall blow the horrid deed in every eye,
> That tears shall drown the wind.[2]

[1] Cf. lines following the soliloquy last quoted.
[2] This passage invariably, even when quoted as here to prove
the contrary, makes me feel that it is Macbeth who is full of
pity ; that the effect on " others " would not be half so great
unless he were there to picture to them how horrid the deed
really was.

And then he seems to regret that he cannot find
more incentives to his villainy :

> I have no spur
> To prick the sides of my intent, but only
> Vaulting ambition, which o'erleaps itself
> And falls on the other.

So Macbeth's searching self-examination on topics
of sin and retribution, amid circumstances specially
calculated to rouse compunction, results in thoughts
no more noble than these—that murder is a game
which two parties can play at, that heartlessness
has the effect of drawing general attention, that
ambition is apt to defeat its own object." [1]

Admitting for the time being the validity of this
method of interpreting character by argument,
what do we find ? We find that there are numerous
other lines which, even if examined with a lawyer's
acumen, could scarcely be interpreted in such a
manner as to obliterate evidence of a strong conscience in Macbeth. If he feels no remorse, why does
he say immediately after the murder of Duncan but
before discovery :

> Wake Duncan with thy knocking ! I would thou
> couldst ?   (II, ii.

Or, consider the first soliloquy in Act III :

> If't be so,
> For Banquo's issue have I filed my mind ;
> For them the gracious Duncan have I murder'd :
> Put rancours in the vessel of my peace
> Only for them : and mine eternal jewel
> Given to the common enemy of man,
> To make them kings, the seed of Banquo kings !
> Rather than so, come, fate, into the list,
> And champion me to the utterance.   (III, i.)

---

[1] Moulton, *Shakespeare as a Dramatic Artist*, p. 150 ff.

It is clear enough that Macbeth feels that he is unsafe and thinks that his actions have been useless if Banquo's issue is to reap the benefit. But he does not simply regret having jeopardized his personal welfare by murder ; he regrets having defiled his mind, having destroyed his peace, and having given his soul to the devil. How can he regret these things if he is not conscious that certain things are dishonourable and do defile the mind, and that he has a soul to sell ?

What does he mean when, in reply to Macduff's " Turn, hell-hound, turn ! " he replies :

> My soul is too much charged
> With blood of thine already ?

What consequences can he fear in killing Macduff —his mortal enemy—except consequences to his soul, the part of man which the conscience is supposed to guard ? And are not the words expressive of remorse for past bloodshed ?

What in the very first instance, when Ross confirmed the first prophecy of the Witches, caused his " seated heart knock at his ribs " ? Was it not the insurrection of all his better instincts against the " horrible imaginings " ?

We cannot but side with Professor Bradley who, after quoting the latter half of the soliloquy beginning " He's here in double trust," says : " It may be said that he is here thinking of the horror that others will feel at the deed, thinking therefore of consequences. Yes, but could he realize thus how horrible the deed would look to others if it were not equally horrible to himself ? "

And lastly, how can the final soliloquy, where life
appears to him as nothing but a " walking shadow "

full of sound and fury,
Signifying nothing,

be interpreted as anything but the despairing cry of
a man whose life had been so filled by misery and
the bitterness of remorse that it had no single
happy moment to offer him ?

Thus we find that the method of analysis used by
Professor Moulton proves that Macbeth had and
had not a conscience. But if you can both prove
and disprove a thing by the same kind of argument
it follows that by argument, or at least by such a
method of argument, the question will never be
settled. We are trying to interpret character, and
this method fails to interpret, because it analyses
each phrase of a dramatic poem as if it were written
in a contract ; it subjects a tragic hero to a species
of cross-examination, objecting to all but a literal
interpretation of his words, but it never thinks to
ask if the audience felt these objections during the
performance of the play. Yet our experience as
spectators or readers is the very thing that has to
be interpreted.

Now let us suppose for just a moment that, in
balancing evidence of the same kind, the evidence
advanced by Professor Moulton is the weightier.
Let us suppose, in other words, that Macbeth's
character when tried by the law-court method—for
that is what the method of argumentation amounts
to—is found to be selfish, shallow, and worthless ;
that Macbeth himself is restrained only by fear of

consequences, and regretful only because his crimes
did not " pay." The conclusion resulting from such
a supposition is obvious : the law-court method is
not a fit method for estimating dramatic character ;
it bids us accept as true that which our experience
as readers and spectators proves to be absolutely
untrue. It interprets the written word, and sums
up character as it could be pieced together from
such words ; but it does not interpret the fact : it
does not interpret our emotion. We actually *feel*
that Macbeth is great, powerful, sublime ; that he
suffers the torments of the damned from an outraged
conscience. Even the critics who reach the conclusion that Macbeth's character is contemptible
admit that the tragedy itself actually rouses our
pity, admiration, and awe ; but it would be impossible for it so to do if we felt and believed Macbeth
to be the man they describe.

We have been sifting the evidence hitherto as
judges—carefully, deliberately, without emotion.
But when we are watching the play we have no time
for deliberation, emotion is everything. Impressions
are made instantaneously, and it is impressions that
count in a play. The above analysis is not a correct
analysis of our impressions and emotions. Macbeth's
scruples and hesitation, the elements of grandeur in
his character, which we coolly brush aside in calmly
estimating the right and wrong of his deeds, all
exert an immense influence on the mind of the spectator. Professor Moulton himself in discriminating
between institutional and individual ethics, in
another place, has brought out very distinctly the
difference between the judge and the spectator :

" The judge may not say to the prisoner : The
burglary of which you have been convicted deserves
a ten years' sentence, but, in consideration of the
magnificent stand you made against the police
while your young comrade was escaping, I reduce
your sentence by one half. The judge would be
more likely to increase the sentence for an additional
offence against social order ; yet the irresponsible
bystander would nevertheless be touched by self-
sacrificing comradeship, and all the more touched
by the fact that it was exhibited in a burglar."[1]

Now we are spectators of Macbeth's magnificent
courage, and we admire it tremendously ; many a
sin could we forgive on account of it. Moreover, we
are not in the position of Macduff and Malcolm who
see only the evil results of Macbeth's action with no
idea of what it cost the man ; we are spectators of
the terrible inner struggle that precedes his first
great crime, and of the excruciating mental
anguish that follows, and our pity goes out to
him as to one suffering as only those can suffer
who have good and great ideals within themselves
to violate.

Although the soliloquy beginning

> If it were done when 'tis done, then 'twere well
> It were done quickly

can be so analysed as to bring about the conclusion
that Macbeth " is regarding the deep considerations
of sin and retribution in no other light than that of
immediate practical consequences," that is not the
impression produced upon the spectators. The

[1] *Shakespeare as a Dramatic Thinker*, pp. 144–5.

spectators believe that the feeling of horror which his words produce in them is what Macbeth himself feels : that his conscience is doing its utmost to withhold him from the deed. For, after all, what is conscience ? It is to be distinguished in the first place from a moral sense based entirely upon reason. A man who always wanted to do right when he recognized it, as for instance Brutus in *Julius Cæsar*, would not be troubled by his *conscience* if he unwittingly chose the wrong path at a turning hard to decide, though he might regret well enough the weakness of his reasoning faculty which had led him into error. It may be disputed as to whether conscience is an instinct, an acquired habit of mind, or divine gift, but all will agree that it is a power or faculty which *warns* us against evil. Now Macbeth certainly had such a faculty ; no man was ever warned of the evil nature of a proposed undertaking more persistently or more clearly than he. But the power of conscience is not preclusive ; a man may do wrong in spite of his conscience, and frequently does. This is where the confusion lies, it seems to me, in saying Macbeth has no conscience. He has a most powerful conscience, but overrides it. He is not, however, always conscious of his conscience. He does not calmly meditate on the right and wrong of a given action and then say he will follow the wrong. But his conscience working through his imagination depicts the wrong in a repulsive light. He overcomes the repulsion simply because his ambition is stronger than his conscience. The reason that so many of the villains that we have hitherto studied seem so unreal and unconvincing is because they

show no signs of the conscience which our experience
in life would lead us to expect in them.

But we do not wish to be one-sided and completely ignore the fact that Macbeth does talk a
great deal about consequences. It may be, and
probably is true that he is moved by thoughts of
worldly prosperity and failure, but the consequences
he fears more than any others are the loss of respect
and honour :

> I dare do all that may become a man
> Who dares do more is none.

He is a nobleman and a great warrior well thought
of by his peers ; he was " once thought honest," and
Macduff "loved him well."   Undoubtedly he was
educated to the conceptions of honour prevalent in
his day ; but he is no Hamlet, speculating on right
and wrong considered apart from current conceptions ; his honour and all his ideas about place and
power are conventional, and he dreads disgrace from
acting dishonourably. This is fear of consequences,
and perhaps it is that only, and yet something might
be said for it as a form of conscience. A soldier feels
his disgrace bitterly if he is dismissed from the ranks
for conduct unbecoming a soldier ; are we not a
little priggish, somewhat casuistical, in saying that
his anguish is not remorse—" in the strict sense "
of the word ?

The fear of losing " golden opinions " may not be
the highest motive for goodness, but it is a very
common motive and by no means to be despised.
It is probably the real motive of a vast majority of
people who to-day profess to govern their conduct by

more metaphysical principles. In the Renaissance, moreover, fame as a motive for conduct was widely defended by poets and philosophers, and was a motive that an audience could sympathize with. Macbeth knows that what he is about to do is dishonourable, yet to gain what he considers the greatest of all honours he is impelled to dishonour, falsely imagining (as the result shows) that if he can hide the dishonour from others it will not trouble himself. He does what thousands of people do daily —except that in Macbeth's case the results are tragic —viz. tries to convince himself, *fools himself*— driven by intense desire—into thinking that he will not regret doing what he at heart knows to be wrong.

But whether the argument identifying conscience with fear of consequences of this kind is sound or unsound, the fact remains that although Macbeth fears consequences he is also horrified, conscience-stricken in the strictest sense of the word, by the terrible pictures which his vivid imagination calls up. In other words, an active conscience is not in the least incompatible with fear of consequences. Macbeth, though a villain, is a tragic figure just because of the struggle with his conscience.

Yet it is worth noting that after the crime, after Macbeth has overridden his conscience, his former courage is temporarily turned into fear of consequences. He fears to return to the chamber of the murdered king. And later he manifests neither conscience nor courage in the slaughter of Macduff's family ; on the contrary, this act is the result of superstitious terror ; it springs from a panicky fear

that his throne is unsafe so long as any of Macduff's
kin are alive. Such superstitious dread, and such
unreasonable fury as Macbeth gives way to after his
first downward step, alienate our sympathy. It is
a matter for wondering admiration that Shakespeare
ever regains it for his hero. This he does, however,
in the last act, by portraying the exquisite
anguish which Macbeth has suffered, and by showing the bed-rock of manly courage beneath
the seeming imaginative softness and impotence
of will shown immediately before and after the
crime.

Two things are necessary to arouse all the tragic
emotions when a villain is the hero of a play : the
hero must have so much greatness in his character
as to call forth our admiration and make us conscious
of the possibilities of human nature ; and there
must be an internal struggle represented. None of
the villain-heroes so far studied has possessed such
greatness except Richard. Barabas showed a touch of
it, but it was soon lost in caricature. Even Richard,
however, proved defective as a tragic hero. Awe
was aroused and we were conscious of the impression
of waste, but we felt no pity for the hero because he
simply used his terrible power to do wrong and never
suffered himself. The other tragic element, the
internal struggle, exemplified in the torments of a
suppressed conscience, was only suggested once at
the close of the play, and its force was not sufficient
to make us feel that Richard's suffering even approximately equalled his deserts. Some kind of an
internal struggle is necessary to arouse pity for a
villain, because in the external action he is injuring

others, which tends to alienate sympathy. But
when that which is good in his own nature, as,
for instance, his conscience, has sufficient strength
to combat his passion, the internal struggle becomes tragic. This is exactly what occurs in
Macbeth.

We all feel that it is not only desirable, but almost
our duty to realize ourselves, to do that which we
can do best. Dramatically speaking, when the self-
realization of a great character injures others or
brings a man into conflict with moral law, then you
have sympathy, tragic pity, because of the element
of greatness in the man. Macbeth is tragic because
he was great and had to realize his greatness, if at all,
through crime. He was fit for kingship and knew it,
and had an overmastering ambition to rule. To
become king he had to commit crime ; yet without
crime he would have remained in a position where
he could not exercise his highest powers. The tragic
dilemma was : " Be unworthy of yourself because
of crime ; or Be unworthy of yourself because of
lack of ambition, of failure to realize yourself."
Shakespeare enlists our sympathies by showing his
fitness for kingship, and by making his only chance
of exercising his powers depend upon crime. We
sympathize with the ambition because we have it
in ourselves ; we are even awed by it because it
develops such a tremendous force in Macbeth ; but
our moral sense compels us to condemn the yielding
to it through the only means that are open. Our
moral sense demands Macbeth's death, and the
satisfaction of the moral sense, Aristotle says, is not
a tragic emotion. But our sense of pity is so stirred

by his mental anguish, our admiration is so great
for his courage, we are so full of awe at the struggle,
that these emotions, which are tragic, counter-
balance the satisfaction of the moral sense, so that
that satisfaction becomes practically the purgative
element which manifests itself by other means in a
tragedy where a good man falls.

There is still another element in this play which
goes to enhance its tragic effect in spite of the fact
that the hero is a villain, and that is the element of
mysterious evil, vague dread, the fear of the unknown, which constitutes the atmosphere of the play
and the effect of which cannot be overestimated.
It seizes upon Macbeth's imagination and colours
his language whenever he thinks of his " black
designs " ; it creates for the spectator a feeling of
both mystery and awe.   Professor Bradley [1] has
called attention to the darkness that seems to brood
over this tragedy ; to the magnitude and violence
of the imagery, such as the babe torn smiling from
the breast and dashed to death, the earth shaking
in fever, and the mind full of scorpions ; to the
unseen forces that seem to be at work independent
of man's consciousness and will : " such as the re-
lapse of Macbeth from conversation into a reverie,
during which he gazes fascinated at the image of
murder drawing closer and closer ; or the sound of
a voice that cried ' sleep no more ' and would not
be silenced " ; to the constant allusions to sleep,
" man's strange half-conscious life " ; and has noted
the fact that " all these agencies—darkness, the
lights and colours that illuminate it, the storm that

[1] Page 333 ff.

rushes through it, the violent and gigantic images—conspire with the appearance of the Witches and the Ghost to awaken horror, and in some degree a supernatural dread." Now such a use of mysterious forces is not only productive of a tragic mood in itself—stirring fear and awe and ultimately impressing us with a sense of tragic waste of power just as in *Richard III*—but by its connection with and influence upon the hero decreases still further the sense of wilfulness already lessened by the internal struggle, and increases our pity for him personally.

Macbeth's own speeches contain many of the images that contribute to the atmosphere of the play. But more than this ; being made by him they seem to show the connection between the evil in his soul and mysterious evil at large. His personal relation with the Witches has the same effect. When he first meets the Witches on the heath and they " hail " him, he seems " rapt." As we have already seen, this points to the presence of evil thoughts already harboured in Macbeth's mind. That the Witches, " secret dark and midnight hags," should hit upon this evil at the very outset and thus at the same time give impetus to his treasonous ambition, seems to point to a secret relation between all things wicked.

The sense of mysterious evil and its relation to Macbeth is again uppermost in that wonderful soliloquy in the first scene of Act II. Macbeth seems to be actually tempted by the dagger which is but the projection of his own heated imagination. As he draws for us a picture of the darkness of the one

half world, so fitting for his present murder, he himself seems to belong to that darkness.

> Now o'er the one half world
> Nature seems dead, and wicked dreams abuse
> The curtain'd sleep ; witchcraft celebrates
> Pale Hecate's offerings, and wither'd murder,
> Alarum'd by his sentinel, the wolf,
> Whose howl's his watch, thus with his stealthy pace,
> With Tarquin's ravishing strides, towards his design
> Moves like a ghost.

And again in Scene 2 he actually seems a part of the
powers he invokes.

> Come, seeling night,
> Scarf up the tender eye of pitiful day ;
> And with thy bloody and invisible hand
> Cancel and tear to pieces that great bond
> Which keeps me pale ! Light thickens ; and the crow
> Makes wing to the rooky wood :
> Good things of day begin to droop and drowse ;
> While night's black agents to their prey do rouse.
> Thou marvell'st at my words : but hold thee still :
> Things bad begun make strong themselves by ill. (III, ii.)

His connection with wrack and ruin, with the
forces that terrify, that seem to be present in his
own nature from the time he resolves upon the
slaughter of Macduff's wife and babes, is felt in his
awful conjuration in the final scene in the cavern
with the Witches while the thunder peals outside.

> I conjure you, by that which you profess,
> Howe'er you come to know it, answer me :
> Though you untie the winds and let them fight
> Against the churches ; though the yesty waves
> Confound and swallow navigation up ;
> Though bladed corn be lodged and trees blown down ;
> Though castles topple on their warders' heads ;
> Though palaces and pyramids do slope
> Their heads to their foundations ; though the treasure
> Of nature's germens tumble all together,
> Even till destruction sicken ; Answer me
> To what I ask you. (IV, i.)

Of this mysterious world of evil the Witches are the visible representatives, "instruments" of darkness. They not only add to the gloomy atmosphere and supernatural setting by their weird incantations and prophecies, but they serve as a connecting link between the evil within Macbeth and the evil forces of nature of which they themselves are but instruments. It has been held that the Witches are symbolic of the evil in Macbeth, but on the contrary, the evil in Macbeth, because of the connection afforded by the Witches, is symbolic of "huge universal powers working in the world of individual fate and passion" and this dilates the imagination so that the individual struggle becomes profoundly tragic. Macbeth's own superstitious nature, the presence of the Witches and the Ghost, the fulfilment of the prophecies, the sleep-walking scene, the reports upon strange things in nature, do not make us believe in "ghosts," or evil spirits, as Macbeth does, but they combine with the murders, with the evil in Macbeth's nature which struggles against the good, to produce in us a feeling that there are strange mysterious forces in nature tending to evil, which sweep a man away with them to his destruction once he exposes himself to their power.[1]

[1] What I have said about symbolism in *Macbeth* and about recognizing the experience of the reader or spectator as authority brings me under Professor Stoll's censure of those critics who read twentieth-century ideas into Shakespeare. (Cf. "Anachronism in Shakespeare Criticism," by E. E. Stoll, in *Mod. Phil.*, Vol. VII, No. 4, April, 1910.) Mr. Stoll believes that we know just what ideas were current in the sixteenth century, and that Shakespeare could not have had any ideas not current in his age. He also believes that it is uncritical to read below the surface of Shakespeare (p. 568), or to trust our emotions if those emotions are based on interpretations of life and action not current in

Neither the Witches themselves nor the more
obscure evil influences which surround a man, according to Shakespeare's conception, actually compel
him to evil. He acts upon his own responsibility.
That is perfectly evident all through the tragedy :
otherwise we might be driven to despair or rebellion.[1]

Elizabeth's time. " The function of criticism," says Mr. Stoll
(p. 557), " is not to make the poet in question the contemporary
of the reader, but to make the reader for the time being a
contemporary of the poet. To criticize is not merely or primarily
to analyse one's own impression of a work of art . . . but to
ascertain if possible the writer's intention and to judge and
measure the force and tendencies of his time. To do this one
must know the author and his time." And again: " There can
be no beauties, still less ideas, foreign to his nature, education,
and time. . . . There can be no artistic effect apart from intention " (p. 574). Admitting that it may be *one* function—the
historic function—of the critic to make the reader a contemporary
of the poet, I am by no means convinced that the function of
interpreting one's own emotion is not equally important. Fur-
thermore, I do not believe, and Mr. Stoll has not proved, that
Shakespeare's ideas were limited to those current in his age,
or, even if they were, that no artistic effect other than what he
intended could exist. The poet sees that an action is dramatic ;
he sees the connection between events ; he may or may not have
a decided opinion as to the relation of such an action to the moral
order of the universe. His artistic purpose is served if he represents the action dramatically. Interpretations of the inner
meaning of the tragedy may vary with the readers' experience
in life. Eighteenth-century critics might interpret the original
action one way, twentieth-century critics another ; if the poet's
imitation of that action in a tragedy indicates an interpretation
of the original action similar to ours, nothing but absolute proof
that he could not have thought as we think will discredit an
interpretation of his meaning which agrees with our conception.
If the dramatist has clearly portrayed the causal relationship
between the events that lead to the catastrophe, what logic will
render unreasonable our attaching as deep a significance to the
tragedy as to the original action of which the tragedy is but an
imitation ? But of the value of making the catastrophe appear
inevitable—an idea as old as Aristotle (cf. *Poetics*, p. 39, Butcher's translation, 4th ed.)—Professor Stoll says Shakespeare
knew nothing. (See p. 572.)

[1] Cf. Schiller's interpretation of the Witches :

Wir streuen in die Brust die böse Saat
Aber dem Menschen selbst gehört die That.

But though every man may act or not and is
responsible for his action, no one can tell what
the results of his actions will be ; they are in-
calculable.   Lear by his hasty temper and one
unwise act brought on a train of evil that extended
far and wide, extinguishing the guilty and the innocent alike.   He could not possibly foresee such consequences.   So with Macbeth : when he plotted the
murder of Duncan he never dreamed that he was
opening the gate to a flood of crime which would
overwhelm all Scotland and ultimately strangle
himself in its waves.   The actual consequences of
that fatal step were as terribly unlike what the hero
anticipated as could be imagined.   He is swept from
one murder to another, driven distracted by care
and remorse, and finally wiped out of existence.
Being predisposed to sympathize with Macbeth on
account of his strength and courage, when he is
tossed about in the grip of these evil forces we forget
to condemn, lost in suspense.   It is as if a man were
to cast himself into the swift waters of Niagara and
then attempt to reach the other shore.   The moment
the swimmer struck out we should cease to pass
moral judgment on his suicidal attempt and watch
with bated breath and high-strung nerves his fearful
efforts to save himself as the current swept him
relentlessly to his doom.

Bringing us face to face with the powers of evil in
the world—which seem just as real as the moral
order itself—connecting man with a kind of Force
within whose grasp he is helpless, lessens the impression of Macbeth's wilfulness, just as Lady
Macbeth's soliciting tends to the same end.   Neither

relieves Macbeth of responsibility, but his wilfulness
seems nevertheless decreased. We feel that he is
just about to give over the murder of Duncan,
horrified at the picture his imagination conjures up,
when Lady Macbeth appears and taunts him with
cowardice. If the reader or spectator were to give
an account of the emotions he feels at this point, I
think he would say that he felt resentment at Lady
Macbeth's interference—sure sign of his sympathy
for Macbeth and belief in the goodness in his nature.
In the same way, but to an even greater extent,
Macbeth's wilfulness is toned down by the impression
of these evil powers. We condemn Macbeth for
his atrocities in the fourth act. Nevertheless,
we feel that he is himself swept along in the
stream of evil which he has let loose. This feeling
becomes more powerful and even merges into
pity in the last act, when the good in Macbeth
reasserts itself.

The prevalence of mystery and the supernatural
serves still another purpose by drawing our attention from the vulgarity of murder and thus preserv-
ing our sympathy for the hero. " Murder," says
De Quincey,[1] " in ordinary cases where the sympathy
is wholly directed to the case of the murdered person
is an incident of coarse and vulgar horror ; and for
this reason, that it flings the interest exclusively
upon the natural but ignoble instinct by which we
cleave to life ; an instinct which . . . exhibits human
nature in its most abject and humiliating attitude.
Such an attitude would little suit the purposes of
the poet. What then must he do ? He must throw

[1] Page 9 ; Variorum ed. of *Macbeth*, p. 138.

the interest on the murderer. Our sympathy must
be with him (of course, I mean a sympathy of com-
prehension, a sympathy by which we enter into his
feelings, and are made to understand them—not a
sympathy of pity or approbation). In the murdered
person, all strife of thought, all flux and reflux of
passion and purpose, are crushed by one overwhelm-
ing panic ; the fear of instant death smites him
‘ with its petrific mace.’   But in the murderer, such
a murderer as a poet will condescend to, there must
be raging some great storm of passion—jealousy,
ambition, vengeance, hatred—which will create a
hell within him ; and into this hell we are to look.”
This effect is to be produced, writes De Quincey,
by insulation. “ The murderers, and the murder,
must be insulated—cut off by an immeasurable
gulf from the ordinary tide and succession of human
affairs.”   The conclusion of his argument is that this
insulation is successfully accomplished and then
suddenly brought to the consciousness of the
audience by the Porter scene, at which time the
reaction sets in.

Insulation does serve exactly the purpose De
Quincey mentions, but it is not the only device used.
The Dagger which Macbeth sees, and sees again,
spotted with blood ; his haunting picture of Nature
dead and witchcraft celebrating, combine with the
atmosphere as a whole to produce just this effect
of taking our thoughts from the vulgarity of murder
and centring them upon the passions which dominate the murderer.

As Shakespeare stirs our sympathy for the hero
by using these devices to modify his wilfulness and

shield him from vulgarity, so he brings out the tragic emotions of pity and admiration by making Macbeth's nature sensitive, capable of deeper feelings than that of the ordinary man. He aspires to greater things, he has greater courage, he has poetic imagination, and through his imagination he suffers more than any other character in the play. He is capable of loving and being loved, but never experiences one moment's happiness. Restive under an unsatisfied ambition, he defies the warnings of his conscience to gain his end, and almost immediately is crushed with despair. When he comes from the chamber of Duncan after the discovery of the murder he utters six sad lines that are intended to deceive, but which nevertheless express his real feelings and are prophetic of the future :

> Had I but died an hour before this chance,
> I had lived a blessed time ; for, from this instant,
> There's nothing serious in mortality :
> All is but toys : renown and grace is dead ;
> The wine of life is drawn, and the mere lees
> Is left this vault to brag of. (II, iii.)

What tortures of the mind are portrayed in the following :

> Better be with the dead,
> Whom we, to gain our peace, have sent to peace,
> Than on the torture of the mind to lie
> In restless ecstasy. Duncan is in his grave ;
> After life's fitful fever he sleeps well ;
> Treason has done his worst : nor steel, nor poison,
> Malice domestic, foreign levy, nothing,
> Can touch him further. (III, ii.)

In the fifth act remorse reaches its highest pitch. Macbeth's anguish is sometimes so intense that he becomes utterly weary of life. Yet this mood alternates rapidly with one of defiance and reckless daring. His experience with life has saddened him but has not lessened his courage, which is more pronounced even than at first.

> *Macb.*   Then fly, false thanes,
> And mingle with the English epicures :
> The mind I sway by and the heart I bear
> Shall never sag with doubt nor shake with fear.
>   (*Enter a servant.*)
> The devil damn thee black, thou cream-faced loon!
> Where got'st thou that goose look ?
>   *Ser.*   There is ten thousand—
>   *Macb.*   Geese, villain ?
>   *Ser.*   Soldiers, sir.
>   *Macb.*   Go prick thy face and over-red thy fear,
> Thou lily-liver'd boy. What soldiers, patch ?
> Death of thy soul ! those linen cheeks of thine
> Are counsellors to fear. What soldiers, whey-face ?
>   *Ser.*   The English force, so please you.
>   *Macb.*   Take thy face hence.   (V, iii.)

When the servant has gone his mood changes to one of world-weariness.

> I have lived long enough : my way of life
> Is fall'n into the sear, the yellow leaf ;
> And that which should accompany old age,
> As honour, love, obedience, troops of friends,
> I must not look to have : but in their stead,
> Curses, not loud but deep, mouth-honour, breath,
> Which the poor heart would fain deny, and dare not.

But as soon as Seyton enters, confirming the servant's report, Macbeth is all daring once more.

> *Macb.*   I'll fight till from my bones my flesh be hacked.
> Give me my armour.

Whenever he has a moment for contemplation, the sad mood forces itself upon him again. Thus when

Seyton informs him of Lady Macbeth's death he exclaims :

> She should have died hereafter ;
> There would have been a time for such a word.
> To-morrow, and to-morrow, and to-morrow,
> Creeps in this petty pace from day to day
> To the last syllable of recorded time,
> And all our yesterdays have lighted fools
> The way to dusty death. Out, out, brief candle !
> Life's but a walking shadow, a poor player
> That struts and frets his hour upon the stage
> And then is heard no more : it is a tale
> Told by an idiot, full of sound and fury,
> Signifying nothing.

Out of this mood of sadness Macbeth is suddenly called by the report that Birnam Wood is approaching. Though staggered by the "equivocation of the fiend," he is in an instant all defiance.

> Ring the alarum-bell ! Blow, wind ! Come, wrack !
> At least we'll die with harness on our back.

Macbeth's last stand is the source of no small element of satisfaction, and contributes to the tragic effect as a whole. The first words we hear about him, before we even see him, are in praise of his bravery. His physical courage is never called in question, but his spiritual courage is not so often recognized, nay, it is even doubted after the murder of Duncan. Yet it is really magnificent. We know that he is superstitious, and that he has an imagination that can call up visions to terrify the boldest ; we know that he foresees the probability of misfortune ; we know that his conscience gives him dreadful warnings ; and yet, with a courage that is terrible, he braves all the evil that his vivid imagination can suggest. And finally, when his very faith

is shaken, when the prophecies of the Witches which
he had counted upon for his very existence are
turned to his destruction and he sees himself a
doomed man, feels himself in the grip of powers that
are crushing him, he defies Fate, the one thing he
actually believed in, and with a magnificent scorn
goes to his death.

> Lay on, Macduff,
> And damn'd be him that first cries ' Hold, enough ! '

It is significant that Macduff is made the instrument of Macbeth's death. Our pity and admiration
for Macbeth have reached their highest pitch by the
time of the death scene ; we forebode his doom but
share his scorn of ordinary antagonists. It would
be unthinkable for Malcolm to defeat him—Malcolm
who fled the country on the first report of his father's
death : he has neither the physical strength nor the
spirit to conquer the tyrant ; it would be distressing
if he did so. Macduff is the only man whose suffering has been portrayed as no less keen than Macbeth's ; the scene where he is told of the death of
his wife and little ones is exceptionally pathetic ;
his agony and the manful efforts he makes to bear it
arouse both pity and admiration. Moreover, he is
represented throughout as noble, courageous, and
absolutely incorruptible ; the only man Macbeth's
equal in bravery, the only one morally his superior,
the only one who, on account of his nobility and
suffering, could draw our sympathy from the hero
in single combat. I think we should rebel if any
other man were permitted to overcome Macbeth.

That Macbeth should finally have justified our
faith in that which was admirable in him, is in the

nature of reconciliation. Reconciliation manifests itself in strange ways in this tragedy. We believe in a moral order ; Macbeth attacks it ; the result is a convulsive reaction. Macbeth spreads suffering far and wide, but he suffers frightfully himself and is finally sacrificed. We are not rebellious or depressed, because the power of goodness, or the moral order, which triumphs is " akin to all that we admire and revere in Macbeth himself." We are conscious at one and the same time of justice and of waste ; the waste is of such magnificent talents, but this impression only produces a sense of mystery ; it is the tragedy of the universe, it does not depress.

We are likewise conscious of justice : I believe with Professor Bradley that we do not *judge* during the action, but at the same time our sense of justice is latent. If the tragedy failed to correspond with the ideas of justice that prevail in our unemotional moments, the effect would be unpleasing, probably morbid. So in a double sense we are reconciled : we are reconciled that the moral order has triumphed, and we are pleased that Macbeth has vindicated in his death our belief in his courage. They are but different sides of the same thing—goodness triumphing in nature and the individual. Perhaps we can carry this sense of reconciliation a little further, to a belief in the sublimity of human nature, a feeling that is more evident in other tragedies than *Macbeth*. It is said that Shakespeare's tragedies always leave us in an optimistic mood because they point to peace following the storm, as, for example, when Fortinbras succeeds Hamlet. And in that sense the same might be said of this tragedy, for with Malcolm, the

rightful heir, succeeding, the way to peace is indicated.   But Macbeth is worth fifty Malcolms :
" What's the boy Malcolm ? "   It increases the
impression of " waste " to feel that a great man like
Macbeth has to give place to a mediocre man like
Malcolm.   But this leads to the other feeling of
reconciliation.   It is the Malcolms who rule calmly
in this world with everyone acquiescing.   Macbeth
is too great for his surroundings.   In this world he
sought the highest place possible for the exercise of
his powers, but he had to attain it by crime.   And
the result of sacrificing the highest and best things
in his nature to material power wrecked his life.   In
gaining the place where he could exercise his powers,
that which was great and good in him, he lost the
means of exercising the powers in a manner har-
monious to his nature.   He came in time to see the
futility of pomp and place ; to see that ambition
only breeds murder, cruelty, pride, contention, and
destruction.   The recognition of the uselessness of
the things he had regarded as most worth while and
which had led him to crime is suggested in the lines :

> I have lived long enough : my way of life
> Is fall'n into the sear, the yellow leaf ;

but is more apparent in the final soliloquy beginning

> To-morrow, and to-morrow, and to-morrow.[1]

It is true these soliloquies do not state directly
that the eternal truths—love, honour, goodness,
beauty—are the only things worth while ; they
only suggest.   But that is Shakespeare's way, he

[1] See supra, p. 215.

never preaches. Macbeth's soul seems to have been
purified through suffering ; at any rate he seems
more noble in renunciation. He has left behind him
both in thought and reality the petty things, the
things that cause most strife in this world, and a
feeling prevails that somehow, sometime, in a world
to come, perhaps, his greatness will have a chance
to realize itself.

This play fulfils all the requisites of great tragedy.
" It is a story of human action producing exceptional calamity and ending in the death of a man of
high estate." A great soul, whose existence fortifies
our belief in the possibilities of human nature, is
presented to our view in a struggle resulting in his
suffering and destruction. The calamities are so
far-reaching, the struggle so intense, the end so
inevitable that admiration, pity, and awe mingle to
produce a tragic effect that is transporting.

CONCLUSION

Our attempt to trace the development of the villain as hero in Elizabethan tragedy here comes to a close. Marlowe seems to deserve the credit for establishing this particular character-type. Before his time there appeared, to be sure, three English plays in which the type may be found, but the authors seem to have been influenced by moral rather than by dramatic motives in selecting wicked heroes, and the plays themselves exerted no influence that can be traced. If Marlowe was influenced by any dramatist, that dramatist must have been Seneca, whose *Medea* and *Thyestes* are typical villain-hero plays. It was the mere fact that Seneca's heroes are villains, however, not the character of the villains, that influenced Marlowe, for Barabas does not resemble Medea or Atreus. Both Tamburlaine and Barabas are typical Machiavellians. Owing to the fact that Machiavelli's writings were creating a great stir at this time, Barabas was at once recognized for what he was, and the violence-loving Elizabethans became fascinated by the guileful and ruthless Jew. Machiavellian villain-heroes at once became popular and ran a long course on the stage. They seem to have been divided into two types, those whose chief motive was revenge, like Barabas, and those whose ruling motive was ambition, like

Tamburlaine. The ambitious type may be traced through Richard III, the perfect Machiavellian, through Macbeth, who is no Machiavellian at all, to Catiline, in whom Machiavellian traits are noticeable once more. The revengeful type runs on through Aaron, Eleazar, Iago, Piero, Hoffmann, Vendici, and Bosola. Machiavellism as a characteristic of the villain-hero begins to die out with Hoffmann ; in Tourneur and Webster's plays it has completely disappeared. No type could be further removed from the egotistical Machiavellian than the subservient tool villain ; yet it is this latter type that Webster raises to the rank of hero. The change here is most significant because the villain becomes heroic by turning good instead of being heroic in his villainy.

Though popular, these villain-hero plays were not as a rule what we would call great tragedies. They failed to arouse any tragic pleasure. Sometimes this failure was due to lack of unity and to sluggish action, as in *Catiline,* sometimes to poor characterization as in *Selimus,* where the hero is unreal ; but more frequently to the kind of character portrayed. As Aristotle foresaw, it is difficult to arouse both pity and fear by a tragedy in which the hero is a villain. We are more likely to hate the hero and regard the catastrophe as mere justice. But Aristotle's doctrine has been found to be not altogether sound : a few villain-hero tragedies do awaken the emotions proper to tragedy, and one— *Macbeth*—is of the very highest order. The first two acts of *The Jew of Malta* are all that could be desired in the way of tragedy, but after this point

Marlowe fails to account psychologically for his hero's actions. Consequently the audience experiences no tragic pleasure in the catastrophe. Shakespeare, however, succeeded where Marlowe failed. He seized upon both the ambitious and revengeful types and psychologized them. Richard, Iago, and Macbeth are all true to life. We may judge from the varying degrees of sympathy aroused by these protagonists what is necessary when the hero is a villain to raise a tragedy to the highest class.

When a villain possesses powers that are great, æsthetically good—such as great courage and great intellectual ability—and when these powers come into conflict with moral forces in the universe so as to produce a struggle which leaves the issue in doubt, we have a tragedy which moves us to admiration, terror, and sadness. When these powers also come into conflict with qualities in the nature of the villain which are morally good, we have a struggle which arouses the highest degree of tragic pleasure, because to the other emotions is added pity for the mental suffering of the hero. Such is the case with Macbeth. When the internal struggle is lacking, as in Richard, the tragedy is not of such a high order because we cannot pity the individual. The emotion of sadness in such a case is due to the loss of great talents, to thinking of what might have been, not to pity for the hero's suffering. When the genius of the villain is less marked, and the internal struggle is also wanting, as in the case of Iago, only the emotion of terror, and that in a modified form, remains. For the highest degree of terror cannot be aroused unless the villain's power of evil is extraordinarily great ; nor can sadness accompany a villain's downfall unless splendid powers perish with him. Though Shakespeare is the only poet who has succeeded in writing a villain-hero tragedy of the highest order, other dramatists, one would think, might attain success if they gave their villain a conscience as well as great powers, and represented the conflict between the greatness and the goodness within him ; if for instance they were to make their villain one who would be good but cannot if he is to give vent to his consuming energies.

APPENDIX A

CHARLEMAGNE

THERE is an anonymous play first printed by Bullen under the title of *The Distracted Emperor* (but called *Charlemagne* by Fleay), which has for its hero a villain. This play is undated, but owing to an allusion by Peele,[1] writing in 1589, to a play by the name of *Charlemagne*, it has been assigned to that year.[2] The play deals with the heroes of Charlemagne romance—Orlando, Oliver, Rinaldo, and Turpin—but the plot is a wretched piece of construction, and the persons are little more than sticks. There are a number of motives, the less and the more important being given equal prominence and attention, while two motives break the unity in the treatment of the hero himself—one of ambition, and the other of friendship.

Ganelon, the hero, appears in Act I plotting for the French throne. He is thoroughly unscrupulous and willing to use any means to attain his end, which fact might suggest Machiavelli. But by the end of the second act he has fallen from favour at court and our attention is then directed to his relations with his friend Richard whom he unjustly suspects of disloyalty. The author seems to have begun with the intention of pro-

---

[1] "A Farewell to Norris and Drake," Bullen's *Peele*, II, 238.
[2] Bullen and Schelling, however, on the ground of style, consider this date too early. Bullen, *Old English Plays*, 1884, III, 161 ; and his note, *ibid.*, II, 421 ; and note 5, *Peele*, II, 238. Schelling, *Elizabethan Drama*, I, 202–3. But cf. Fleay, II, 319.

ducing a Machiavellian intriguer on a basis of French romantic history, but to have become absorbed as he progressed with the problem of representing the emotions of a distinguished man, fallen from power, and deserted by his best friend. This break in the plot is not, however, the worst feature of the play. In his efforts to win the throne Ganelon makes use of a magic ring by the properties of which he gets the emperor in his power. The foundation of the action upon such an impossible situation makes any serious consideration of the play impossible.

APPENDIX B

THE MERCHANT OF VENICE (1596)

So much has been written about *The Merchant of Venice* that a modern critic can hardly hope to add anything new, but in forming an estimate of the play may side with one critic or the other, or form an eclectic judgment based upon the sum total of opinions. Some critics consider *The Merchant of Venice* a tragedy, others call it a comedy ; some think Shylock is the hero, others say he is not. There is no doubt, however, as to Shylock's villainy. His character has even certain points in common with the type villain-hero. He is revengeful like Barabas,[1] but he is not a monster, nor is it his startling deeds which hold our attention. There are, indeed, certain traces of Machiavellism in his language. For instance, we learn in the third scene of the first act (I, 110), that he, like Barabas, is patient under injury. He is also a religious hypocrite (IV, i, 227–8). But, as Meyer points out, " he neither murders by underhand means, nor dissembles, nor poisons as Barabas does ; in short, he is much less even of an Elizabethan Machiavellian. To the audience, perhaps, his most Florentine trait was his great wealth and covetousness, which idea had been introduced by Marlowe."

It is perfectly clear that Shylock is not one of those villains who step to the front as dramatic heroes simply

[1] His relation to Barabas has been so completely set forth by Ward (*Hist. Eng. Dram. Lit.*, I, 347) that it would be idle to attempt a detailed distinction here.

226

because the diabolical cleverness of their villainy over-
shadows everything else. On the contrary, if Shylock
is the hero it is because we sympathize with him so
much for his suffering. The difficulty of deciding upon
Shylock's position is closely interwoven with the problem of whether the play is to be treated as a tragedy or
a comedy. If it is the latter, Shylock cannot possibly
be the hero; if it is the former, his position is not so
easily determined. The trouble all centres in the character of Shylock, and comes to a head in the fourth act.

The difficulties that confront us, however, in interpreting the play probably had no existence for Elizabethan minds. Hatred of the Jews was so pronounced
in Shakespeare's day that the audience of that time
probably had no particle of pity for Shylock. His
hardness of heart was a matter for hatred, his misfortune a matter for jeers. His suffering was not an occasion for sympathy, but a sign of degradation : i.e. anyone who could be spat upon must deserve it. So ran
the popular judgment.[1] Even to-day there are some
readers of *The Merchant of Venice* who regard Shylock as
a villainous Jew unworthy of pity even when most deeply
humiliated. But the majority of men of the twentieth
century sympathize with Shylock. They feel that the
wrongs which he has suffered account for his conduct. He
is kicked into the gutter by those who are stronger than
he, and then reviled for bearing the marks of his harsh
treatment. How can he help hating his tormentors ![2]

[1] See E. E. Stoll's article entitled "Shylock" in *The Journal
of Eng. and Ger. Phil.*, Vol. X, No. 2, 1911.

[2] I cannot agree with Professor Stoll that unless we regard
Shylock as a humorous character as the Elizabethans did we
are reading something into Shakespeare that is not there. If
Shakespeare presents Shylock's point of view so accurately that
without changing a word we of to-day feel the justice of his
complaint and see the hypocrisy of the Christians, I see no reason
why we should not credit Shakespeare with seeing what he makes
us see, even though his contemporaries were blinded by prejudice
and brutal by nature.

But all our sympathy cannot change a play technically constructed as a comedy into a tragedy. The
trial scene is tragic and the character of Shylock is
tragic, but this does not transform the whole play.
Even for the Elizabethans the fourth act must have
been tense because Antonio comes so near death. But
the situation is happily resolved (according to the
Elizabethans' way of thinking), which fact would con-
firm them in their acceptance of the play as a highly
romantic comedy. Even upon our minds the other
scenes and the two minor plots, which are conceived
in a lighter vein, produce an effect of comedy which is
not to be obliterated by the tragic elements.

If, however, we were to consider the main action
alone, ignoring the sub-plots, would not Shylock be
the hero ? And would not the play then satisfy the
demands of tragedy ? The surest way to answer these
questions is to outline the story from the standpoint of
the Jew as protagonist :

A Jew who hates a Christian plots to get rid of his
foe without endangering his own life. He therefore
loans him money upon a bond which provides for the
forfeiture of a pound of the Christian's flesh if the money
is unpaid by a certain date. The Jew is about to vent
his hatred by enforcing the bond when he discovers
that the enforcement will result, by legal process, in
his own death. He therefore cancels the bond and re-
treats defeated and deprived of his wealth.

Such is not the main action in *The Merchant of Venice*.
It presents the story in an entirely different light.
Shylock, the villain of the play, suffers a tragic fate,
but that does not make him the hero, any more than the
fact that Creon, in Sophocles' *Antigone*, suffers tragi-
cally in the loss of his son and wife makes him the hero
of that play. Creon plays a very important part in the
action ; he makes a tyrannous decree and enforces it

by ordering Antigone to be buried alive. When he learns what is likely to result from this sentence he hastens to relieve her, but arrives too late. He loses in his son and wife all that made life dear to him—a tragic fate. And yet if anyone were to attempt to present this as the main action, the higher and what as a matter of fact is the really absorbing tragedy of Antigone herself would be lost. A tragedy might be written with Creon as the hero, just as a tragedy might be written with Shylock as the hero, but in that case the effect of the respective plays would not be what it now is. Shylock might then be made to inspire terror just as Richard and Barabas do. So far, however, are we from thinking that he can crush his virtuous enemies that we pity the poor Jew in spite of his villainous attempt at retaliation.

If Shakespeare had elaborated the character of Antonio as carefully as he has that of Shylock there would be no doubt as to who was intended as protagonist. As it is, Antonio is rather neglected for the sake of the love story. He is good and is well loved by his friends, but he is not so characterized that we love him as his friends do. Our interest in his welfare is that which we have for a man whom we know to be deserving ; it is not the interest of personal attachment. With the Jew, however, Shakespeare has adopted methods just the reverse. All the decent people in the play hate him. But in spite of this fact, and in spite of the fact that he is actually a usurer, the poet makes us sympathize with him by revealing his proud and spirited inner nature, and by displaying the oppression which has brought about the hardening of his character. But by doing this he has simply made us sympathize with his villain ; he has not made him the hero.

On the other hand, Antonio fits into the main action as hero very well. It is the merchant whose life is put in jeopardy by a noble action. It is he for whom we

are concerned. It is he who is about to suffer unmerited misfortune, and his danger stimulates both
pity and fear for the time being. Our pity for Shylock
begins long before the fourth act and is not due to any
danger he is in of losing his life, but the pity we feel
during the trial scene is aroused by Antonio. Yet at
the end of the play we are not in that serious mood
that accompanies tragedy. This is undoubtedly due
to the fact that Antonio has escaped misfortune
and that there are no deaths. But this is to say
that although Antonio is the hero the play is not a
tragedy.

Indeed, we ought not to expect a tragic ending if
Antonio is the hero, for his character is untouched by
tragic guilt. If we consider Aristotle's doctrine of pity
and fear for a moment the truth of this statement will
be apparent. Aristotle says that the spectacle of a
virtuous man—one not guilty of error or frailty—brought
from prosperity to adversity " moves neither pity nor
fear ; it merely shocks us." What the character of the
ideal hero of tragedy should be we have already discussed in another place. Now, Antonio is too good to
be a tragic hero ; his character is that of the virtuous
man just mentioned. He shows no frailty in signing
the bond ; on the contrary, he manifests nobility of
nature in taking such a risk for a friend. This generous
act is not at all an error of a noble nature, but evidence
of a noble nature. That is why a really tragic ending
in the fourth act would be impossible. The balance
does seem to waver. At first it seems as though Shylock
might be allowed to take his pound of flesh and go free.
Even after the appearance of Portia it is just possible
that he might sacrifice his own life to drag Antonio
down with him. But the balance only seems to waver ;
there is really no likelihood of its going down on the
wrong side. Consider for a moment the effect upon our

emotions if Shylock were to kill Antonio. Would our
emotions be tragic ? No. We should simply be shocked.
The play would be read once and never again. Such a
contract as was made between Shylock and Antonio is
extremely artificial ; its artificiality is passed over
without criticism owing to the prevalence of the atmosphere of comedy ; but were such a bond pressed to its
fatal conclusion its essential artificiality would manifest
itself and condemn the whole play. The effects of an
error like Lear's are felt to be consequential, but the
laws of any country that would permit life to be for-
feited upon such a bond as that drawn in *The Merchant
of Venice* would be monstrous, and the imitation on the
stage of an action representing such a sacrifice would
be monstrous, not tragic.

We might designate *The Merchant of Venice* a tragi-
comedy, if we knew what a tragi-comedy was. If we
could accept Professor Schelling's definition of this
hybrid all would be well. " The truest tragi-comedy,"
he says, " is that which trembles between a tragical and
a happy solution, as do the later acts of *Measure for
Measure*, or *The Merchant of Venice* in that supreme
moment when Shylock elects submission, though freely
offered his heart's revenge."[1] Yet, because those plays
which are unhesitatingly classed as tragi-comedies all
contain very distinct flaws in dramatic workmanship,
these flaws, rather than the trembling of the balance
between tragic and happy solution, have come to be
regarded by the less critically minded among readers
as the distinguishing feature of tragi-comedy. These
" besetting sins," as Schelling calls them, " are false
sentiment and a sacrifice of dramatic logic to surprise,
perverted ethics, and an overthrow of the laws of cause
and effect." [2] Now, these flaws are not characteristic

[1] *Elizabethan Drama*, Vol. II, 183.
[2] *Ibid.*

of *The Merchant of Venice*. Although our feeling at the
end of the play amounts to neither the serious mood
that accompanies tragedy (as we have already explained)
nor yet (owing to the pity we still feel for the unfortunate Jew) that lively satisfaction usually experienced
upon the resolution of a skilfully wrought comedy, this
result has nothing to do with the besetting sins of tragi-
comedy.   Antonio's release from threatened death is
quite logical and does not overthrow the laws of cause
and effect. It might, if the freeing of Antonio depended
upon the quibble of not letting a drop of blood in the
operation of extracting the pound of flesh. But this
quibble of Portia's is merely put in for dramatic effect.
It is dramatic to see the tables turned so squarely that
Shylock is defeated in his bond by the very letter of the
law through which he thought to enforce it. But the
situation here is altogether too tragic to be satisfac-
torily resolved by a quibble. Shylock has violated the
spirit of the law which forbids murder. He has attempted to take the life of Antonio and at the same
time avoid punishment for the crime. Shakespeare
makes this attempt at murder a crime by Venetian law,
and Shylock suffers for his crime. There is no sacrifice of
dramatic logic here. If we were judging the trial scene
in the play as we should a real trial instead of by its
dramatic power, we should unhesitatingly accuse the
Duke and all of Antonio's friends, as well as the lawyers
of Venice, of the most hopeless stupidity not to have
thought of this law and cited it as soon as the trial
opened. By making the defeat of Shylock's criminal
purpose finally turn upon this reasonable law, the dramatist satisfies our sense of justice and still permits us
to retain our sympathy for the Shylock as a down-
trodden Jew. Shylock's very yielding is logical, for
with all his vindictiveness and proud spirit, and in spite
of the fact that during the excitement of the trial we

are nervous as to the outcome, we feel at the close that Shylock would never have been willing to sacrifice his own life to gain his end.

From what has been said it follows that *The Merchant of Venice*, if a tragi-comedy, is such not because of the sacrifice of dramatic logic to surprise but because, as Professor Schelling says, it "trembles between a tragical and a happy solution." Whether such a trembling of the balance is the logical distinction between tragi-comedy and romantic comedy, however, is a question.[1]

Yet even as tragi-comedy, Antonio remains the hero. In fact, Shylock can only be made the hero of *The Merchant of Venice* if we consider it a soul tragedy and ignore the force of the outward action. If we refuse to take notice of the part played by Antonio as a generous man, willing to run the risk of death to oblige a young lover, and consider the play simply as the representation of the mind or soul of an oppressed but proud-spirited Jew who longs with all the intensity of his passionate soul to get his oppressor beneath his foot, and who, when on the verge of success, depending upon the impartiality of the law—the only thing that does not oppress him— is at that moment caught by that very law and subjected to still deeper humility ; then, I say, if we regard this soul struggle as the essence of *The Merchant of Venice*, Shylock is the hero. But otherwise not. As other motives in the play cannot be ignored, however, and as other characters have our sympathy, we are forced to conclude that *The Merchant of Venice* is not a tragedy and that Shylock is not the hero.

[1] Professor Schelling himself discusses *The Merchant of Venice* in his chapter on Romantic Comedy.

APPENDIX C

MEASURE FOR MEASURE (1603-4)

OF all Shakespeare's plays *Measure for Measure* seems
to have produced the most unsatisfactory results.
This is due, I think, to the imperfect amalgamation of
comic and tragic elements. The play is undoubtedly
a comedy in construction, and yet it contains scenes
and motives that are tragic. It would be uncritical to
say that the comic and the tragic could not be brought
together successfully in one play, but the fact remains
that their fusion is imperfect in *Measure for Measure*.

In this one play there are three tragic motives : the
conflict of law with individual ethics ; trial of woman's
chastity ; and the conflict of self-sufficiency with
temptation. Behind them all is the comic motive of
the disguised Duke. Disappointment results because
the comic motive is used to solve the tragic problems.

The Duke's leniency in the first place breeds disregard
for law, but disregard for a law that was too severe to
be executed. It needed amendment, not enforcement.
Consequently Angelo's enforcement of it works injustice.
When he refuses to temper justice with mercy we get
the first tragic situation. Immediately following comes
Angelo's own crime—not his disregard for chastity, but
his abuse of a public trust, his threat to punish Claudio
unless Isabella submits to his wishes. Though everyone recognizes that the statutory penalty is too severe
for Claudio's offence, Angelo's crime is deserving of the
full rigour of the law. It also entangles the tragic

situation. But how is this situation resolved ? By overthrowing the laws of cause and effect. The Duke pardons both offenders and marries the real criminal to a very lovable woman—punishes him by heaping coals of fire on his head, as it were. If such a resolution proves anything, it is not, as has been suggested, that laws are useless as moral restraints, but that such governors as Angelo and the Duke are inefficient.

This is what we feel when we allow our serious feelings to get the upper hand. But considering the comic setting nothing else was possible. As Knight says,[1] had Angelo been adequately punished the catastrophe would have been even more unsatisfactory. The reason is not only that the Duke has meddled in the whole affair, deceitfully permitting Angelo to show his character, while preventing harmful results, thus depriving himself of a just right to punish Angelo, but that Mariana has helped the Duke and Isabella out of a very embarrassing situation, and claims Angelo as her husband for a reward. To allow her to marry such a criminal is shocking, but to cause her suffering by killing Angelo would be the height of injustice.

As for the trial of Isabella's chastity, it also has become tragic. After she breaks out in passionate denunciation of her brother, the situation calls for serious treatment. Will she show a greater regard for her chastity or for her brother's life ? She is not compelled to decide, but is saved by a ruse.

Moulton[2] has a paragraph on " motive form " as applied to tragedy and comedy which is most instructive in handling the problem of *Measure for Measure*. He feels that the terms *comedy* and *tragedy* are inadequate when applied to Shakespeare. " The distinc-

[1] C. Knight, *Studies of Shakespeare*, ed. 1849, p. 320.
[2] R. G. Moulton, *Shakespeare as a Dramatic Artist*, p. 372 ; published Clarendon Press, 1906, 3rd ed.

tion these terms express is one of Tone, and they were
quite in place in the Ancient Drama in which the comic
and tragic tones were kept rigidly distinct and were
not allowed to mingle in the same play. Applied to a
branch of Drama of which the leading characteristic
is the complete Mixture of Tones the terms necessarily
break down, and the so-called 'Comedies' of *The
Merchant of Venice* and *Measure for Measure* contain
some of the most tragic effects in Shakespeare. The
true distinction between the two kinds of plays is one of
Movement, not Tone. In *The Merchant of Venice* the
leading interest is in the complication of Antonio's
fortunes and its resolution by the device of Portia.
In all such cases, however perplexing the entanglement
of the complication may have become, the ultimate
effect of the whole lies in the resolution of this complication ; and this is an *intellectual effect of satisfaction*. In
the plays called Tragedies there is no such return from
distraction to recovery : our sympathy having been
worked up to the emotion of agitation is relieved only
by the emotion of pathos or despair. Thus in these
two kinds of dramas the impression which to the
spectator overpowers all other impressions, and gives
individuality to the particular play, is this sense of intellectual or of emotional unity in the movement : is,
in other words, Action-Movement or Passion-Movement.
The two may be united, as remarked above in the case of
The Merchant of Venice, but one or the other will pre-
dominate and give to the play its unity of impression."

The fault with *Measure for Measure* is that, although
it unites both Action-Movement and Passion-Movement,
the union is brought about simply by jamming them
into the same play, instead of fusing them. The entanglement of the complication is so perplexing that
the resolution does not resolve. The Duke lays a nice
little plot to test both Angelo's character and the effect

of a vigorous administration. This is comedy, for the audience accompanies this Haroun-al-Raschid on his adventures. Such fearful complications result, however, both from the unjust enforcement of law and the criminal development in Angelo's character that the Duke is forced to plot anew to counteract the evil he has let loose by retiring from the throne.

This is the crux of the action. It is barely possible, though not probable, that such a serious situation as that in which Isabella and Angelo find themselves might be turned into comedy by some ingenious device by the Duke that would expose Angelo to ridicule and scorn ; or the situation might be saved for pure tragedy. But the result is neither pleasant comedy nor serious tragedy. The device which the Duke adopts is questionable not only morally but dramatically, because, while increasing Angelo's guilt,[1] it demands an artificial resolution. The Duke's solution of the difficulty is entirely inadequate. It is not calculated to restore a respect for law, nor is it in the slightest degree appropriate to Angelo's wickedness. Our sense of justice is outraged. Hence the intellectual effect produced by a skilful resolution of the complication, and proper to Action-Movement or comedy—viz. satisfaction—is wanting. On the other hand, our " sympathy having been worked up to the emotion of agitation " is *not* relieved by the emotion of pathos or despair. A " return from distraction to recovery " is attempted, but unsuccessfully. Hence we are also deprived of tragic emotion.

As *Measure for Measure* is a comedy, and the full play of Angelo's villainy clogged by comic machinery, an instructive comparison of his characteristics with those of the villain-heroes of *bona fide* tragedy is hardly possible. He is cruel, hypocritical, lustful, and shrewd.

---

[1] Angelo later breaks his promise, imagines he is violating Isabella, and actually does break the statute on chastity.

Cruelty, hypocrisy, and shrewdness are traits possessed by Machiavellians, but do not distinguish the type, as almost any villain is likely to have such characteristics. His lust, however, is not Machiavellian, nor a common trait of the villain-heroes. Piero is lustful, but is not the same kind of a villain. The nearest approach to Angelo aside from the hero of the play of *Promus and Cassandra*, on which *Measure for Measure* is founded, is Appius in the old play of *Appius and Virginia*. The motive of a tyrant and apparently just judge being incited to lust by a virgin and using the power of his office to subject her to his desires is the same in both. As Angelo does not, however, carry out his wicked intention, but is safely married off, we are unable to tell just what the effect on our emotions would have been had the play been constructed as a tragedy retaining the villain Angelo as hero. Considering the nature of his villainy, it is doubtful whether we could have felt any sympathy for him. Still, it is possible. A few lines are given to Angelo in which he soliloquizes upon the surprise which his own nature has given him in falling a prey to sensuality. And in the end he asks for death as a release from shame. But an exhaustive treatment of these two motives is not attempted. Had Shakespeare chosen to depict more clearly the moral struggle before the fall, and the dejection after it, he might have touched our sympathies. But in that case it would have been necessary to omit the Mariana incident, because Angelo's previous treatment of her shows his nature to be fundamentally mean and cowardly, two traits a knowledge of which in advance would make the moral struggle appear ridiculous.

APPENDIX D

APPIUS AND VIRGINIA

By Webster (pr. 1654)

ONE other play dealing with the theme of woman's chastity, though of uncertain date, and printed (1654) long after the period under discussion, may be mentioned here, because it was written by Webster, one of whose plays we have already treated, and because it relates to an early Elizabethan tragedy of the same name which has already been discussed. Webster's *Appius and Virginia* is more powerful and more artistic than Bower's [1] play. In the early tragedy Appius was not introduced until after our sympathies had been won by Virginia, and consequently was rendered more subordinate than he should have been in a play in which he was supposed to be the protagonist. Moreover, the didactic purpose made prominent by the Morality figures was rather adverse to æsthetic enjoyment. In Webster's play, however, Appius is foremost on the stage, and takes his place at once as technical hero. His character is contrasted with that of Virginius, who suffers much more intensely than his daughter. Virginia is kept in the background, comparatively speaking, and her suffering is relieved by the martyr's crown.

The first scene reveals Appius' character almost in its completeness. He is a cunning, unscrupulous

[1] *Appius and Virginia* (1575), by R. B. See *supra*, p. 23.

239

politician, who would exploit the state without giving one whit of honest service in return. His character as politician is also his character as private citizen—shrewd, unscrupulous, selfish, and tyrannical. Withheld by no moral scruples, he will satisfy his lustful desires provided he can do so without injury to his reputation. He is selfish enough to be hated, too powerful to be held in contempt, yet not passionate enough to be pitied, nor bold enough to be admired. In fact, he possesses no admirable qualities other than those which have served the ambition of many an unscrupulous man, such as astuteness, will-power, and a certain amount of courage. He is forceful but not mighty; shrewd but not sagacious. There is nothing likeable about him, nothing great. Nothing becomes his life so well as the leaving of it. In the final scene he displays bravery in meeting death, but no greater bravery than might be expected of any Roman of his training. That which lends greatest dignity to the character of Appius is the noble character of his enemy, Virginius, who has to bear the brunt of his villainy.

We admire certain scenes in the play, but we cannot class the tragedy among the best. The hero arouses no sympathy: he is far too hypocritical and base. We pity only his victims. Some satisfaction is felt in his death, but no profound depths in human nature are sounded by either his life or death. An unjust judge who never had our sympathy meets with well-merited retribution.

APPENDIX E

THE INDEX OR TABLE OF *MACHIAVELS* MAXIMES, CONFUTED IN THOSE DISCOURSES, DIVIDED INTO THREE PARTS

The Maximes of the first part doe handle such Counsell as a Prince should take

1. A Princes good Counsell ought to proceed from his owne wisedome, otherwise, he cannot be well counselled.

2. The Prince, to shun and not to be circumvented of Flatterers, ought to forbid his friends and Counsellors, that they speake not to him, nor counsell him anything, but only in those things whereof he freely begins to speake or asketh their advice.

3. A Prince ought not to trust in Strangers.

.   .   .   .   .

The Maximes of the second part, handling the Religion which a Prince ought to observe, and be of

1. A Prince above all things ought to wish and desire to be esteemed Devout, although hee be not so indeed.

2. A Prince ought to sustaine and confirme that which is false in Religion, if so be it turne to the favour thereof.

3. The Paynims Religion holds and lifts up their hearts and makes them hardy to enterprise great things : but the Christian Religion, persuading to Humilitie humbleth and too much weakeneth their minds, and so makes them more ready to be iniured and preyed upon.

4. The great Doctors of the Christian Religion, by a great ostentation and stiffenesse have sought to abolish the remembrance of all good letters and antiquitie.

5. When men left the Paynim Religion they became altogether corrupted, so that they neither beleeved in God nor the Divell.

6. The Romane Church is cause of all the calamities of Italy.

7. *Moses* could never have caused his lawes and ordinances to be observed, if force & arms had wanted.

8. *Moses* usurped Iudea, as the Gothes usurped a part of the Empire.

9. The Religion of *Numa* was the chiefe cause of Rome's felicitie.

10. A man is happy so long as Fortune agreeth to his nature and humour.

.　　.　　.　　.　　.

The Maximes of the third part, entreating of such Policie as a Prince ought to have

1. That Warre is just, which is necessary : and those Armes Reasonable, when men can have no hope by any other way but by Armes.

2. To cause a Prince to withdraw his mind altogether from peace and agreement with his adversarie, he must commit and use some notable & outrageous iniurie against him.

3. A Prince in a conquered countrey must establish & place Colonies and Garrisons, but most especially in the strongest places, & to chase away the naturall & old inhabitants thereof.

4. A Prince in a country newly conquered, must subvert & destroy all such as suffer great losse in that conquest, and altogether root out the blood and race of such as before governed there.

5. To be revenged of a Citie or countrey without striking any blow, they must be filled with wicked manners.

6. It is folly to thinke, with Princes and great Lords, that new pleasures will cause them to forget old offences.

7. A Prince ought to propound unto himselfe to imitate *Cæsar Borgia*, the sonne of Pope *Alexander VI.*

8. A Prince need not care to be accounted cruell, if so be that he can make himselfe to be obeyed thereby.

9. It is better for a Prince to be feared than loved.

10. A Prince ought not to trust in the amitie of men.

11. A Prince which would have any man to die, must seeke out some apparent colour thereof, & then he shall not be blamed if so be that he leave his inheritance & goods unto his children.

12. A Prince ought to follow the nature of the Lyon and of the Foxe, yet not of the one without the other.

13. Cruelty which tendeth and is done to a good end, is not to be reprehended.

14. A Prince ought to exercise cruelty all at once ; and to do pleasures by little & little.

15. A vertuous Tyrant, to maintaine his tyrannie, ought to maintaine partialities & factions amongst his subiects, and to sley and take away such as love the Commonweale.

16. A Prince may as well be hated for his vertue, as for his vices.

17. A Prince ought alwaies to nourish some enemie against himselfe, to this end, that when he hath oppressed him, he may be accounted the more mighty and terrible.

18. A Prince ought not to feare to be periured, to deceive, and dissemble ; for the deceiver alwaies finds some that are fit to be deceived.

19. A Prince ought to know how to wind and turne mens mindes, that he may deceive and circumvent them.

20. A Prince which (as it were constrained) useth Clemencie and Lenitie, advanceth his owne destruction.

21. A wise Prince ought not to keep his faith, when the observation thereof is hurtful unto him, and that the occasions for which he gave it, be taken away.

22. Faith, Clemencie, and Liberalitie, are vertues very damageable to a Prince : but it is good, that of them he only have some similitude and likenesse.

23. A Prince ought to have a turning and winding wit, with art and practise made fit to be cruell & un-faithfull, that he may show himselfe such an one when there is need.

24. A Prince desirous to breake a peace promised and sworne with his neighbour, ought to move warre against his friend, with whom he hath peace.

25. A Prince ought to have his mind disposed to turn after every wind and variation of Fortune, that he may know to make use of a vice, when need is.

26. Illiberalitie is commendable in a Prince, and the reputation of a handycraftsman, is a dishonour without evill will.

27. A Prince which will make a strait profession of a good man, cannot long continue in the world amongst such an heape of naughtie and wicked people.

28. Men cannot be altogether good nor altogether wicked, neither can they perfectly use crueltie and violence.

29. He that hath alwaies carried the countenance of a good man, and would become wicked to obtaine his desire, ought to colour his change with some apparent reason.

30. A Prince in the time of peace, maintaining dis-cords and partialities amongst his subiects, may the more easily use them at his pleasure.

31. Civile seditions and dissensions are profitable, and not to be blamed.

32. The meanes to keep subiects in peace and union, and to hold them from Rebellion, is to keep them alwaies poore.

33. A Prince which feareth his subiects, ought to build fortresscs in his country, to hold them in obedience.

34. A Prince ought to commit to another those affaires which are subject to hatred & envy, and to reserve to himselfe such as depend upon his grace and favour.

35. To administer good Iustice, a Prince ought to establish a great number of Iudges.

36. Gentlemen which hold Castles and Iurisdictions are very great enemies of Commonweales.

37. The Nobility of France would overthrow the Estates of that Kingdome, if their Parliaments did not punish them, and hold them in feare.

BIBLIOGRAPHY

THE following is a list of the critical works to which reference is made in the foregoing chapters :—

Aristotle. *Poetics :* ed. by S. H. Butcher. 4th edition. Macmillan, London, 1907.

Ascham, Roger. English works : ed. by W. A. Wright. Cambridge University Press.

Baker, G. P. *The Development of Shakespeare as a Dramatist.* Macmillan, New York, 1907.

Boas, F. S. *Shakespeare and His Predecessors.* Scribners, New York, 1906.

Bradley, A. C. *Shakespearean Tragedy.* Macmillan, London, 1908.

Briggs, W. D. *Influence of Jonson's Tragedy.* Anglia, XXXV ; N. F. B., XXII. 1912.

Bullen, A. H. *Works of Peele.* London, 1888

Burckhardt, Jacob. *The Renaissance in Italy.* Trans. by S. G. C. Middlemore. Sonnenschein, London, 1909.

Burd, L. A. (editor). *Il Principe.* Clarendon Press, Oxford, 1891.

Butcher, S. H. *Aristotle's Theory of Poetry and Fine Arts, with a Critical Text and Translation of The Poetics.* 4th ed. Macmillan, London, 1907.

Campbell, Lewis. *Tragic Drama in Aeschylus, Sophocles, and Shakespeare.* Longmans, Green & Co., New York. Smith, Elder & Co., London, 1904.

Cellini, Benvenuto. *Autobiography.* Trans. Everyman's Library. Dutton.

Churchill, G. B. *Richard the Third up to Shakespeare.* Palestra, X.

Collier, J. P. *Shakespeare.* London, 1853.

Courthope, W. J. *Hist. Eng. Poetry* (V. II, c. I., on Machiavelli). Macmillan.

Croll, M. W. *The Works of Fulke Greville.* Pennsylvania Thesis, 1903. Printed Lippincott, Philadelphia.

Cunliffe, J. W. *The Influence of Seneca on Elizabethan Tragedy.* Macmillan, 1893. Stechert, N.Y., 1907.

De Quincey, Thomas. *Collected Writings:* ed. Masson, Vol. X. London, 1896.

Dickinson, T. H. Introd. Mermaid edition of Plays of Robert Greene.

Dowden, E. *Shakespeare : His Mind and Art.* Harper and Bros., London; New York.

Einstein, Lewis. *The Italian Renaissance in England.* Macmillan, 1907. Columbia University Press.

Fields, Baron. Edition of *True Tragedy of Richard III.*

Fleay, F. G. *A Biographical Chronicle of the English Drama,* 1559–1642. London, 1891.

Fleay, *A Chronicle History of the London Stage,* 1559–1642. London, 1890.

Gairdner, James. *History of Life and Reign of Richard III.* Cambridge University Press, 1898.

Gentillet. *Discours sur les Moyens de bien gouverner et maintenir en bonne paix un Royaume ou autre Principauté : Divisez en trois Parties : à savoir, du Conseil, de la Religion et Policie que doit tenir un Prince : Contre Nicholas Machiavel, Florentin. A Treshaut et Très-illustre Prince François, Duc d'Alençon, fils et frère de Roy.* 1576.

Greville, Fulke. *Life of Sidney.* The Fuller Worthies Library. Ed. A. B. Grossart, 1870.

Hazlitt. *Characters of Shakespeare's Plays.* London, 1817.

Hudson, H. N. Preface to Aldus ed. of *Richard III.*

Janet, P. *Histoire de la science politique dans ses rapports avec la morale.* Paris, 1887.

Kellner, L. " Die Quelle von Marlowe's *Jew of Malta.*" Eng. Stud. Vol. X.

Knight, C. *Studies of Shakespeare.* London, 1849.

Liddell, M. A. *Macbeth.* The Elizabethan Shakespeare. Doubleday Page, New York, 1903.

Macaulay, T. B. *Machiavelli.* Critical and Historica Essays, Vol. I.

Machiavelli, Niccolo. *Historical, political and diplomatic writings.* Tr. from the Italian by C. E. Detmold. Boston, 1882. (4 v.).

Meyer, Ed. S. *Machiavelli and Elizabethan Drama.* Literarhistorische Forschungen, I.

Miller, F. J. *The Tragedies of Seneca.* University of Chicago Press. Unwin, London, 1907.

Mohl, Robert von. *Die Geschichte und Literatur der Staatswissenschaften.* Erlangen, 1855-8.

Moulton, R. G. *Shakespeare as a Dramatic Artist.* Clarendon Press, Oxford, 1906.

Moulton, R. G. *Shakespeare as a Dramatic Thinker.* Macmillan, 1907.

Nietzsche, Friedrich. *The Will to Power.* Trans. and ed. by Dr. O. Levy, 2 vols. Macmillan, London, 1910.

Noyes, G. R. *Aristotle and Modern Tragedy.* Mod. Lang. N., 1898.

Patericke, Simon. *A Discourse upon the Means of Well Governing and Maintaining in Good Peace a Kingdome or Other Principality.* Printed by Adam Islip, London, 1608.

Plutarch. *Lysander.* Works: ed. Langhorne. Cincinnati, 1866.

Rees, Kelley. *The so-called Rule of Three Actors in the Classical Drama.* Thesis. University of Chicago, 1908.

Schelling, Felix. *Elizabethan Drama.* Houghton Mifflin Co., Boston and New York, 1908.

Simpson, R. *The Political Use of the Stage in Shakespeare's Time; The Politics of Shakespeare's Historical Plays.* New Shak. Soc. Vol. I.

Stoll, E. E. *John Webster.* Monograph. Mudge and Son, Boston, 1905.

Stoll, E. E. *Anachronism in Shakespeare Criticism.* Mod. Phil. Vol. VII, No. 4, April, 1910.

Stoll, E. E. *Shylock.* The Journal of Eng. and Ger. Phil. Vol. X, No. 2, 1911.

Symonds, J. A. *Shakespeare's Predecessors.* London, 1884; new ed., 1906.

Symonds, J. A. *The Italian Renaissance in Italy—Age of the Despots.* N.Y., 1881.

Thorndike, A. H. *Hamlet and Contemporary Revenge Plays.* Pub. Mod. Lang. Ass.

Thorndike. *Tragedy.* Houghton Mifflin, 1908.

Vaughan, C. E. *Types of Tragic Drama.* Macmillan, London, 1908.

Villari, Pasquale. *The Life and Times of Niccolo Machiavelli.* Translated by Linda Villari. London.

Wallace, C. W. *The Children of the Chapel at Blackfriars.* Lincoln, Nebraska, 1908.

Ward, A. W. *History of English Dramatic Literature.* Macmillan, 1899.

INDEX

AARON, see *Titus Andronicus*

Acomat, see *Selimus*

Agamemnon, not a villain-hero play, 14; revenge in, 100

Alaham, influence of Machiavelli, 69–70; influence of Seneca, 70; compared with *Œdipus* and *Medea*, 71; compared with *Selimus*, 69; lack of tragic emotion in, 70–1;

Alaham: an ambitious villain-hero, 68; characteristics, 68; a Machiavellian, 69; compared with Selimus, 70; emotions aroused by, 70–1; compared with Sejanus, 172

Alcmæon, referred to, 13

Alexander VI, Pope, character of, 11
  See also Devil's Charter

Almanzor, compared with Selimus, 67

Ambition, in *The Jew of Malta*, 60; as a motive for action, 60–1; not the *sine qua non* of Machiavellism, 99

Anderson, Pastor, 7

Angelo, see *Measure for Measure*

Antigone, conflict of the heroine with law, 4–5; Antigone, not Creon, the protagonist, 228–9; compared with *The Merchant of Venice*, 228–9

Anti-Machiavel, nature of the book, 33–4; source of Machiavellism, 33
  See also Machiavelli

Antonio, see *Antonio's Revenge ; Merchant of Venice*

Antonio and Mellida, date, 133

Antonio's Revenge, revenge-for-a-father type, 133; two types of avenger in, 134; Antonio's revenge justifiable, 134; two protagonists, 135–6; influence of Gentillet's maxims, 137; influence of *The Prince*, 137; no tragic emotion aroused by, 139–40; melodramatic elements in, 140–1;
  compared with: *The Spanish Tragedy*, 103, 133; *The Jew of Malta*, 103; *Othello*, 133;
  Piero: mixed type, 103; descended from Barabas and Aaron, 103; the hero, 134, 136; part equals Antonio's in importance, 135; revengeful Machiavellian villain, 221; tragic career, 135; Machiavellian traits, 136–8; character revealed in soliloquy, 136–7; depravity, 116; lustfulness, 138–9; no admirable traits, 139; motives for conduct, 136; revenge unjustifiable, 134, 136; emotions aroused by: repulsion, 139–40:
  —— compared with: Aaron, 133, 138; Atreus, 114, 138; Barabas, 138; Bosola, 103; Eleazar, 133, 138; Iago, 116, 133; Lorenzo, 103, 134, 137; Medea, 114, 138; Vendici, 103, 149

Iago, *see Othello*

Italy, influence on Elizabethan drama of, 11–12

Jew of Malta, The, significance as villain-hero play hitherto unnoted, 2 ; popularity, 2 ; source of, 9–10, 44 ; hero a Machiavellian, 39 ; value of soliloquies in, 53 ; motives in, 60 ; rank as tragedy, 221 ;

    compared with : *Tamburlaine,* 8–9 ; with *Thyestes,* 45 ; with *Selimus,* 65 ;

    Barabas : as Superman, 9 ; prototype of the revengeful Machiavellian villain-hero, 51, 102–3, 221 ; emotions aroused by, 52–9, 85 ; degeneration of, 57–9, 222 ; influence of Lorenzo upon, 100–1 ; influence on later villain-heroes, 101–3 ;

    —— character : 2, 8, 39, 41–2, 47–61, 101–3, 220 ; Machiavellian traits, 39, 41–2, 47–51, 60, 101, 220 ; admirable traits, 53–6 ; ambition and revenge, 60 ;

    —— compared with : Lorenzo, 41, 44, 51 ; Tamburlaine, 60–1 ; Selimus, 67 ; Richard III, 79, 81, 84–5 ; Hieronimo, 102 ; Aaron, 105, 107–8 ; Atreus, 108 ; Eleazar, 111–3 ; Iago, 134 ; Piero, 138 ; Hoffmann, 144 ; Vendici, 148–9 ; Bosola, 162, 164 ; D'Amville, 167 ; Sejanus, 177 ; Macbeth, 192, 203 ; Shylock, 226 ;

    —— nature of his revenge : unjustifiable, 102, 134 ; distinguished from that of Hieronimo, 101–2 ; of Aaron, 106, 108, 134 ; of Atreus, 108 ; of Eleazar, 134 ;

    influences affecting the creation of : spirit of the times, 10–12 ; Seneca, 44–6 ; Machiavelli, 45–51 ;

    influence of : general, 60–1, 79, 102–3 ; on Richard III, 79 ; on revengeful villain-hero type, 99, 103

    —— *See also names of plays*

    tragic emotion in : 52–9, 85, 221–2 ; cause of weakness in last three acts, 57, 59, 221–2

Jews, attitude of Elizabethans towards, 227

Jocasta, not a villain-hero play, 21

Jonson, mentioned, 99 ; influence of Machiavelli upon, 171

    See also Sejanus ; Catiline

Justice, in *Macbeth,* 217

King Lear, tragic " waste " in, 93 ;

    compared with : *The Duchess of Malfi,* 160 ; *Richard III,* 98 ; good and evil in, 116

    Goneril and Regan : villains, 4 ;

    Lear : character, 6, 87 ; consequences of his frailty, 210 ; mentioned, 231

Kyd, Thomas, influence of Seneca upon, 99 ; influence upon villain-hero plays, 99 ; influence on Marlowe, 100–1

    See also Spanish Tragedy

sadness, 213–5; sensitiveness, 213, 217; superstitious, 202–3, 215; wilfulness, 188, 210;
—— compared with: Barabas, 192, 203; Eleazar, 192; Hoffmann, 192; Richard III, 192, 203, 221;
—— conscience: 192, 193, 195, 196, 197, 200, 202, 204, 215;
Macbeth, Lady: Influence on Macbeth, 190–1, 211;
Macduff: significance of his being the instrument of Macbeth's death, 216;
tragic emotion in: admiration, 198–9, 205, 213, 215–6, 219; awe, 198, 205–6, 219; pity, 198, 204–5, 213, 216, 219, 222; fear, 206; effect of the presence of mystery and the supernatural, 205–12, 217; "waste," 206, 217–8; effect of Macbeth's last stand, 215–6; satisfaction of the moral sense as "Katharsis," 205, 217–8; justice, 217
Machiavelli, life of, 31; denounced by Catholics and Protestants, 32–3; denounced by Gentillet, 33, 36; cause of influence on dramatists, 38–9; influence of Seneca upon, 42–3; popular belief that he was under the control of the devil, 51; Massacre of St. Bartholomew attributed to influence of, 72; doctrines distorted by Gentillet, 102; table of maxims arranged by Gentillet, 241ff;
influence on: tragic drama, 10, 60–1; Cambridge students, 37; Gabriel Harvey, 36–7; Greene, 37; Marlowe, 37, 220; *The Spanish Tragedy*, 40, 42–3, 137; *The Jew of Malta*, 45–6, 48–51, 60–1; Barabas, 49–51; *Tamburlaine*, 60–1; *Selimus*, 68; *Alaham*, 70; *Massacre at Paris*, 72; *True Tragedy of Richard III*, 76; *Richard III*, 79–81; *Titus Andronicus*, 103; *Lust's Dominion*, 103; Iago, 103; *Antonio's Revenge*, 136–8; Jonson, 171; *Sejanus*, 171; *Catiline*, 178
See also *The Prince*; Machiavellism; Gentillet; *names of plays and characters*
Machiavellians, ambitious and revengeful types, 220
Machiavellism, the result of Gentillet's *Anti-Machiavel*, 33–4; distinguished from the doctrine of Machiavelli, 47; Gabriel Harvey's contributions to, 47; in *Othello*, 123; melodramatic appeal of, 138; in *The Devil's Charter*, 183–4; disappearance of, 221
characteristics: 41–3, 47–50, 60–1, 66, 99, 101–2, 114, 134, 138, 178; ambition, 99; revenge, 99, 101–2, 134, 138; disregard of human life, 102; cruelty distinguished from cruelty of Seneca's villains, 114; revenge different from revenge of Seneca's villains, 134; lust not a characteristic, 138; malice, 138; affectation, 178
See also Gentillet; Machiavelli; Patericke; *names of plays and characters*
Mamillia, quoted to illustrate the term Machiavellian, 37
Marlowe, Christopher, influence upon romantic drama of, 1–2; character, 9; compared with Nietzsche, 9; establishes villain-hero type, 29, 220; influence of Machiavelli upon, 10,